Nature in Needlepoint

Designs by Eva Brent

Text by Meg Merrill

Simon and Schuster · New York

For Si and Michael with love—Meg
To Mother, for helping me get started—Eva

Stitching Credits:

*Male and Female Lion Heads, Lynda Gillam; Lion Cub in Octagonal
Border, Jean Ochert; Resting Male Lion (partially stitched), Jeri Schatz;
Resting Tiger, Elaine Rich; Tiger Cub with Bee, Roslyn Wechsler; African
Elephant with Baby, Meg Merrill; Pair of Zebras, Jane Brooks; Two
Giraffes with Acacia, Meg Merrill; Monkey Mother and Infant, Kay Gordon;
Two Rabbits with Violets, Roslyn Wechsler; Eagle on a Crag, Meg
Merrill; Two Owls on Two Branches, Jannie Lim; Swans, Ruby Burleson;
Birds with Red Border, Meg Merrill; Birds with Orange Border, Jeneane
Pearlman; Four Ducks with Flowers at Stream's Edge, Joan Wooley; Frog
with Lily Pads, Meg Merrill; Grasshoppers on Flowering Branches,
Jeneane Pearlman.*

Published by Simon and Schuster
A Gulf + Western Company
Rockefeller Center, 630 Fifth Avenue
New York, New York 10020

Designed by Beri Greenwald
Graphs and drawings by Libra Graphics, Inc.
Color photographs by George Senty and Clara Aich
Manufactured in the United States of America

3   4   5   6   7   8   9   10

Library of Congress Cataloging in Publication Data

Brent, Eva.
  Nature in needlepoint.

  Bibliography: p. 125
  *1. Canvas embroidery—Patterns.   2. Design,
Decorative—Animal forms.   I. Merrill, Meg.   II. Title.*
TT778.C3B73   746.4′4   75-16129
ISBN 0-671-22081-1

Acknowledgments

THIS BOOK could not have been written and designed without the devoted help of many friends, associates and relatives who gave untiringly and, usually, uncomplainingly of their time and knowledge. They are too numerous for us to list completely, but there are some whose generosity makes it imperative that we mention them by name.

To Beri Greenwald and her staff of artists at Libra Graphics, Inc., who executed the graphs and, with patient good humor, made change after change after change, we owe our deepest gratitude.

To Joe and Dorothy Davis, who shared with us their incredible store of animal expertise, we owe the accuracy of our facts regarding wildlife.

Of all the people who helped put this book together, the most significant to Eva have been Jeneane Pearlman, Joan Hansel, Doris Budner, Marilyn McAtee, Joan Wooley, Roslyn Wechsler and Lynda Gilliam from *The Needle in a Haystack* store, Dallas, Texas. Efficient, caring and punctual, untiring in their efforts in stitching many of the pieces for this book, they came through at the eleventh hour, as did Evelyn C. Vanston and Barbara Taylor, who blocked and finished many of the pieces. Thanks, too, to Kay Tornborg.

Special thanks from Meg go to Stewart Rawlings Mott, who once needed a present and thus inspired the desire to learn needlepoint, and to Barbara Brown, patient teacher and good friend.

And, finally, with a deep sense of obligation and with affection, we must mention Julie D'Alton Houston, our editor, and Harriet Ripinsky. Their help, encouragement and patience went far beyond any requirements of duty.

EVA BRENT and MEG MERRILL

Contents

Chapter Five

An Appreciation of Wildlife

WOLVES USED TO LIVE in my native New Jersey. Pumas used to live there, too. Tigers used to live throughout millions of square miles of tropical and temperate Asia. Sea otters used to live along almost all of the western coast of North America, from Baja California to the far Aleutian chain, and over into the waters of northern Asia. So many kinds of animals "used to live" in vast areas of the earth from which they are now gone. Too many just "used to live," and live no more, anywhere in this world. Nor will their species ever live again.

The common factor in the diminution and disappearance of animals is that creature we call *Man,* when we are too pedantic—or too ashamed—to use the word *us.* We are the only species ever known to have totally destroyed another species or race—unless one counts the cat that wiped out an entire small population of island-dwelling wrens. But the cat was brought to the island by a lighthouse keeper, and as a species our list of extinct victims numbers over two hundred in the last four centuries, with more than six hundred kinds of birds and mammals lining up, or rather, being lined up, for inclusion in the not-distant future. There are some who argue that Man is just another natural force, like changing climate or movement of the planet's crust, and that man-made extinction is no more to be mourned, or stopped, than the forces that have shaped earth's living things since time began. If true, the extinction we dole out is the result of the first natural force that is consciously controlled, and the first that can be stopped and reversed. What *Man* has done is less important by far than what *we* can do.

Biologists can offer strong reasons why it is our species' own selfish interest to keep alive as much of our world's diversity of living things as we can. We can continue to get along without the dodo, it seems, and maybe we can survive without the tiger. But if we persist in herding living things into extinction we may well perish with our victims. The reasoning behind this utilitarian argument for conservation need not be detailed here. This book is an eloquent argument in itself for another selfish reason to secure the future of wildlife. Nature in all its expressions is beautiful, and nowhere is it so beautiful as in its animal forms. The earliest known human artistic expression involves the depiction of animals. Like painting and sculpture, the needlepoint designs in the following pages are an outgrowth of a deep-seated human urge to portray the beauty of nature. If for no other reason than to inspire our love of beauty we ought to preserve our natural world. Yet, beautiful as our portrayals of animals are, these graphic works can never be more than imitations of life.

JOSEPH A. DAVIS
General Curator
North Carolina Zoological Park

ARTISTS HAVE BEEN FASCINATED with the living world around them, right from the moment when the cavemen first decorated walls of their cavern homes with pictures of animals painted with natural vegetable dyes. Down through the centuries, there exist magnificent examples of natural subjects not only painted with brushes on canvas and paper, but also worked on fabrics with needles and strands of wool, silk, cotton, gold and silver. Both real and imaginary animals have been stitched on wall hangings, pillows, rugs, fire screens, articles of clothing, book jackets, chair seats, entire coverings for chairs and needlework paintings. In fact, the list of things that can be made with petit point, needlepoint or gros point is endless and bounded only by the imagination.

While there is nothing new about nature in art or needlepoint, a new awareness of today's environment has created a worldwide resurgence of interest in both nature and needlepoint—and in the two combined. All animals, not excluding man, have a nest-building instinct. As our world has become more and more computerized, machine-made, compressed and crowded, a natural desire to create pieces of personal art with which to decorate our nests has emerged. Although it may not be a conscious awareness, the more we live in brick and steel, the more we destroy and push aside the sight and smell of flowers, trees, birds and animals, the more we miss their presence. It is not by accident that apartments are becoming tiny gardens with plants in every corner, on every shelf and even hanging from ceilings, nor is it any surprise that more and more people are finding joy in needlepointing the vanishing world of nature into pieces of art for their homes.

Chapter One

General Information, Materials and Supplies

Because most needlepoint can be carried in a small bag and used to pass the endless hours spent in traveling and relaxing at home, some may think of it as no more than a simple handicraft. When the designs are worked with style, wit and care, however, it is far from being either simple or a handicraft. Needlepoint is an art form as well as a hobby. As an art, it is challenging, time-consuming, expensive, sometimes tedious (filling in backgrounds and ripping mistakes) but always, if it is done with care, very rewarding. Needlepoint pieces are practically indestructible and visually beautiful; they become heirlooms to be cherished through generations.

Although basic instructions for needlepoint stitching and designing are included, this book was not conceived as a ''how-to'' book, but rather as a pattern book for Eva Brent's wildlife designs. There are many excellent books available that concentrate on presenting in detail the many stitches and techniques that can be used on the canvas, and the bibliography gives the names of some of them. The addresses for suppliers of canvas, yarn and accessories are given as well.

Eva's naturalistic designs have been deliberately drawn for both the beginning and the advanced needlepointer. The simplicity or intricacy can be determined by the size and kind of canvas used, by the number of colors used, and by the stitch variations.

MATERIALS

Canvas

Canvas is the fabric, or woven base, on which the needlepoint stitches are formed. The best canvas is made of cotton or linen and comes in white and various shades of pale tan, ecru, or beige. Try to avoid canvas made of synthetic threads. It is less expensive but the small saving in money is not a saving when you consider the amount of man- or woman-hours involved in stitching a piece of needlepoint. New canvas is sized and feels stiff, but it will become pliable as you work it. Synthetic canvas is uncomfortably hard when new and then becomes completely limp and lifeless. Do not buy canvas that has knots, bumps or broken threads. Always check.

Canvas is composed of warp (vertical) and woof (horizontal) threads.

The threads cross each other at regular intervals to form an openwork pattern resembling wire screening. The openings are called meshes. Single-mesh canvas is called mono—that is, it has only one thread between meshes. Double-mesh canvas is called Penelope (*see illustration*)—that is, paired threads form the mesh. These can be separated to allow for small stitches, making it possible to use two different stitch sizes on the same piece of work.

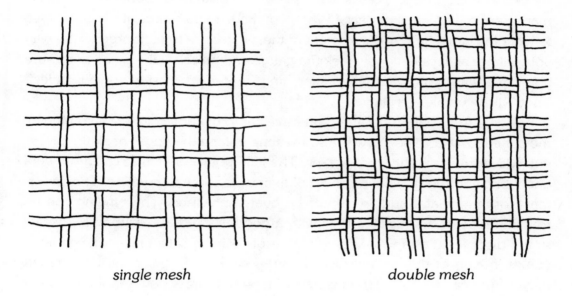

single mesh   *double mesh*

The thread count, or number of meshes to the inch, gives the size of the canvas. This is called the gauge. Therefore, the gauge of canvas having 10 meshes to the inch is number 10 in mono. Penelope canvas in this size would be number 10/20. Canvas comes in an almost unlimited number of gauges, from that which is almost a fine gauze down to 3 stitches to the inch. The very lowest gauges are called Quick Point and will not concern us here. The designs in this book can be adapted to canvas between gauges 8 and 18. The gauge of the canvas will determine the size of the finished piece and the number of stitches per inch.

Each square in a needlepoint graph represents one stitch. For example, if you want to make a pillow on number 10 canvas and the design is 100 stitches by 100 stitches, you will need a working area of 10 inches square on a piece of canvas cut 14 inches by 14 inches. This includes an extra 2 inches of canvas all around for blocking and seaming. In measuring, always add this 2-inch border to your working area.

Canvas is usually sold by the yard, and most stores will not sell less than half a yard. Canvas comes in a variety of widths from 18 inches to 54 inches, but not all gauges come in all widths or all colors. Often you will have to buy a piece somewhat larger than you need. After cutting it to the size you need, do not discard the remainder even if it seems to be a scrap. Small pieces make handy bits on which to practice new stitches, and some scraps are large enough for pincushions, eyeglass cases, baby pillows, Christmas tree ornaments, bookmarks, and other small projects. When you have extra scraps, it is a good idea to write the gauge and measurement of the piece close to the border. That way you will not always have to check the gauge and measure the piece to be sure you have what you want when searching for canvas to start a new project. They will be visible at a glance.

The first thing to do after you have cut your canvas to size is to bind all the cut edges with tape. Now is also the time to tape the edges of all the pieces you will store, even the small scraps. The little points of canvas catch on wool and fabric and seem to have a mind of their own about unraveling. The importance of immediate binding cannot be overemphasized. The binding can be masking tape or any flexible tape with a good, sticky back. During a hospital stay, I discovered a tape made by Minnesota Mining called Hypoallergenic. It comes in a small roll—1 inch by 10 yards—and works perfectly. Lay the cut edge of the canvas halfway on a strip of tape and press down. Fold the other half of the tape to the other side of the canvas and again press. Secure it by pulling your fingers across it a few times. You need not bind the selvage edge.

Preprinted Canvas

Obviously canvas with the design already painted on is more expensive than plain canvas, but the designs are frequently beautiful, and you may find one that is exactly what you like. They can be easily modified to suit your decorative scheme. Colors can be changed, leaves or flowers can be added or deleted, an interesting border can encircle the design, a plain background can become stripes or squares, or one with a design too busy for your taste can be stitched in a solid color. Decorative stitches in solid areas will add their own texture and design. Do not feel that your work is valueless if you have bought a preprinted canvas, but also have the courage to transfer your own favorite designs to canvas (*see chapter 5*).

Frames

One of the nice things about needlepoint is that, unlike embroidery, it does not need to be worked in a frame. This is true in all cases, but there are times when a frame can be helpful. If you are making a rug that becomes heavier and heavier with every stitch and can't be carried around unless you are the Jolly Green Giant, a standing frame will help take the weight off your legs. Also, an enormous piece of needlepoint lying in your lap in the summer will begin to make you feel as though you are tending a small furnace.

Yarn

Almost any wool or thread can be used in canvas embroidery, as needlepoint is sometimes called. The type will be determined by the use to which you will put your work. Obviously, a rug requires more durable yarn than a petit point picture or even a large wall hanging. For small areas of special colors, you can use knitting wool if it has a flat—that is, not fuzzy—appearance. Knitting wool and crochet cotton are not suggested for large areas, as they are too fragile to withstand the constant strain of pulling back and forth through the canvas. The best length to cut your yarn is approximately 36 inches; however, delicate strands should be somewhat shorter and heavy strands can be a little longer.

There is no hard-and-fast rule for deciding on the amount of wool you will need. The stitch used, the tension you use when you work, and the number of times you need to rip are all considerations. To get an estimate, work a one-inch square in the stitch you will be using. Be sure to do it on the same size canvas that you intend to use. Note the length of yarn you have used in inches and the approximate number of inches you will need to cover with that color. Multiply one by the other, and you will have the number of inches of yarn needed. You can easily convert that into yards. Although most needle-point yarn is sold by weight, if you give the shop the amount of yarn in yards, they will convert it to weight for you. Be sure to keep in mind that if you split your yarn and use one or two strands, you will need less yarn; if you add a strand, you will need more.

If you have drawn your design on canvas, there is a fairly simple way to determine the number of inches of each color you will need. On a sheet of acetate, which you can buy in any art supply store, draw one-inch squares. If you use indelible ink, you will be able to use the pattern over and over. If not, your hands will smudge the lines and you will eventually have to make another one. Tape the sheet over your canvas, and you will easily estimate how many inches, half-inches or fractions of inches you need for each color. If you give this information, together with the canvas gauge, to the shop, they will be able to determine how much yarn is needed.

It is always better to buy too much wool than too little. Matching dye lots, while not as difficult as it once was, is not always possible. There is often the tiniest variation in color, which is not visible until it is worked on the canvas, when it becomes a major disaster, especially if you are unable to obtain any more of the old dye lot. In any event, most shops have a minimum amount they will sell, and you might end up having to buy the extra amount you would have bought in the beginning. Also, a cache of bits and pieces of leftover wool will come in handy when you need just a few strands of one or another color for accent in a later design.

The gauge of canvas will determine the thickness of yarn needed. If you find that a dark color is not covering completely, try loosening your tension or adding another ply. If, no matter what you do, you still see white specks of canvas through the dark wool, you can color in the area with indelible paint or marker (*see chapter 5*). If the threads of your canvas begin to distort, or if, after you have worked an area, you have trouble pulling your wool through the meshes, the wool is too thick. It should slip through easily. Try subtracting a ply, and that should eliminate the problem.

On the opposite page is a list of canvas gauges and the wools that match them. Use it only as a guide. Your tension and the particular stitch you are using may call for adjustment in the number of strands.

Paternayan Persian Wool

This is imported wool which is dyed in the United States. The wool is three-ply, that is, three strands with the plies loosely woven, and is easily separated into one, two or three strands. Therefore you can add strands for wide-mesh canvas, subtract them for fine-gauge or mix more than one color for a tweedy or shaded effect. There are 336 Paternayan colors. Most of the colors

CANVAS GAUGE	YARN	CANVAS GAUGE	YARN	CANVAS GAUGE	YARN
Number 10	3-ply Persian 4-ply tapestry	Number 14	2-strand Persian 2-strand crewel 6-strand DMC cotton 4-strand silk	Number 18	1-strand Persian 1-strand crewel 4-ply DMC cotton 4-ply silk
Number 12	2-strand Persian 2-strand crewel 6-strand DMC cotton 6-strand silk	Number 16	1-strand Persian 1-strand crewel 4-ply DMC cotton 4-ply silk		

within this group range in gradations, or schools, of from three to seven shades. This wool has a bright, almost silvery sheen. If you cannot find a shop that carries Paternayan wool, you may write to them (*see Sources for Supplies and Professional Finishing),* enclosing a stamped, self-addressed envelope; they will give you the names and addresses of stores near you. If you need a color that is not in their stock, they will custom dye wool, but there is a small dye charge and you must order a minimum of five pounds of wool. You can do this only through the shop with which you deal. There are approximately forty-four yards per ounce. The wool is mothproofed, as are almost all wools now.

You can also buy Paternayan canvas. The gauges are number 10 through number 18 in mono and number 5/10 through number 12/24 in Penelope.

Crewel Wool

This is two-ply wool made expressly for crewel, but it works equally well for needlepoint. The plies can be separated, in Persian wool for example, so they can be combined for heavy canvas or divided for petit point. The colors are bright with a glowing sheen. In Paternayan Brothers crewel wool, there are 252 shades. Often you can find a color that will blend between two shades of Persian wool if you are trying a particularly delicate blending of color. It does not cover quite as well as Persian, especially in the dark colors, and the strands are not as uniform in size. You may have to adjust your tension or use three instead of two plies.

DMC Cotton

This thread comes in 330 colors, which are beautifully shaded and blended. The colors are brilliant and shiny. It is a six-strand thread, but with care the threads can be separated for addition or subtraction. It can be used with or in place of silk, and it is easier to work with and less expensive. I have seen glorious pillows made with a center design of DMC cotton and the background in Persian wool. It is more difficult to keep the cotton strands even and untwisted than it is with wool, but this is not an insurmountable problem.

Tapestry Wool

This is four-ply wool that can be divided only with great effort and some damage to both the wool and your temper; so, unless there is a color that you absolutely must have and cannot get any other way, it is best to use it as it comes from the skein. It comes in a wide color range that is almost without peer if you want delicate shading. It also has the advantage of being available in small amounts, so that, if you need a few stitches in one color, you do not need to buy much more than necessary. There are 324 DMC tapestry colors.

Silk

This is expensive thread and somewhat more difficult to work with than the others. The strands are delicate and tend to snag and bunch easily. The colors have a lustrous, polished look. Silk is extremely effective for highlighting small features, such as the eyes, nose, and claws, of an animal.

Metallic Thread

Gold and silver metallic threads are both very expensive and very difficult to use. They have a slippery feel, and great care must be taken to have each stitch match the others. It must be used in short lengths, as it tends to unravel easily. Both ends should be securely woven into the underside of the canvas. Always experiment with metallic thread before making any sizable investment in it.

SUPPLIES

Needles

The proper size needle is important for even stitching. A too-large needle will force the canvas out of shape and will be hard to pull through the meshes; a too-small one will fray the wool. There is, however, a certain flexibility in needle sizes. Following is a list of the proper needles for the canvas:

CANVAS GAUGE	NEEDLE
3 through 5	13
7 through 8	15
10 through 14	17 or 18
16 through 18	19 or 20
20 through 32	21 through 24

Because individual needles do not come with the size marked on them, I have found it convenient to keep at least one needle in the original package with the size marked on it. That way you can always check your needle size against one you know is correct. Canvas embroidery needles have blunt points, although the higher needle sizes will have proportionately sharper points. The blunt point is important for two reasons; to keep the needle from pricking your finger and to prevent you from splitting your wool or canvas, neither of which should you ever do—the first because it hurts and the second because it is unsightly. To thread the needle, make a small loop at one end of the wool and hold it firmly between your thumb and forefinger. Slide the needle through this loop, pulling the wool tight. You can then easily push the doubled end through the large eye of the needle. If the wool will not go through or frays as you thread the needle, try the next larger size. The best needles are Scovill, an American brand, or Boye, made in England.

Thimble

Some people do not use thimbles. I find that if I do not, I eventually manage to work a small, painful hole in my finger. Thimbles come in various sizes and many designs. Those with a hole in both ends are useful for people with long fingernails and are cooler in summer. Try thimbles on until you find one that fits tightly enough not to slip off constantly but is not so tight that it will stop your blood circulation. Also, even though you may be tempted to get a fancy thimble with stones set into it, resist the impulse. The little points that hold the stones will snag your wool.

Scissors

Needlepoint scissors should be small, sharp, and have fine points. Invest in a good pair. Use them only to cut your wool and never for cutting canvas or paper, which will dull the blades. They should stay razor sharp.

I keep a small, heavyweight plastic purse in the bag with my work, and it contains the following:

Scissors

Thimble

Small emery board   Even a tiny rough spot on your nail will snap at your wool.

Small bag of sand   These are available at almost any place that sells sewing materials or notions. It is an invaluable aid when your needle begins to feel sticky or rough, as it will with continued use. When the needle turns gray instead of shiny silver, push it back and forth in the sandbag a few times, and it will immediately regain its original slippery feel.

Extra needles   It is very frustrating to start to work only to find that your needle has disappeared. It once happened to me at the start of a ten-hour plane trip and it will never happen again. The little plastic cases that pills come in are marvelous needle cases, and you can mark the needle size on the top.

Pair of sharp-pointed tweezers   Often, after you have removed some stitches, you will want to replace them with a different color. If you do not pick out all the fuzz, you will have a subtle shading where you do not want it.

A nifty, new organizer designed for the traveler is called a Point Pack, and the name describes its function perfectly. The Lucite holder keeps wool neatly arranged and when it is closed there is a canvas strap with snaps around it to hold the wool in place. It fits into the canvas bag with room left for your work, and there is a pocket for your little bag of accessories. The Point Pack can be ordered by mail from Schaefer Designs, 158 Duchaine Boulevard, New Bedford, Massachusetts 02745. It costs $24.95.

Chapter Two

Stitches,
Basic Rules
and Techniques

BEFORE EVA PAINTED THE ANIMALS, birds and insects from which the canvases in this book were designed, careful research was done in museums, libraries and zoos. One of the hardest jobs was trying to decide which animals to select among the thousands of living creatures, each with its own particular beauty and merit, and conversely which to leave out. Space and time were determining factors in the choices we finally made. We know there are many we have not included that are excellent subjects for needlepoint, but we hope that the ones we have chosen and the instructions for stitching them will spur our readers into doing their own original wildlife designs.

When completed, each design in this book will resemble a painting—executed with needle and wool rather than with paints and brushes. They can all be completed beautifully using two basic stitches, and these are the only ones for which directions are given. Experienced needleworkers may include more complicated stitches for additional texture and pattern, but these are not necessary to the elegance of the finished work.

Regardless of which stitches you use, if you have never done needlepoint, you will want to practice them on a small piece of canvas before you begin to work a design. This will help you learn the rhythm of stitching and the tension needed for even designs.

STARTING A STRAND

To start your first stitch, tie a knot at the end of your yarn. Push your needle from the front through to the back approximately an inch directly

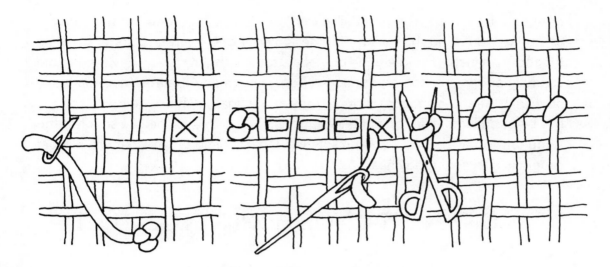

first stitch and knot anchoring yarn

to the left of the mesh which will be your first stitch. This leaves the knot on the front of the canvas (*see diagram above*). Bring the needle back to the front at the point where you will begin your first stitch. The inch-long piece of wool in the back will be covered by stitches as you continue to work and will anchor your wool securely. When you reach the knot, clip it off from the reverse side of your work. This will prevent little frayed threads from showing through the design. You need to do this only when you are starting to work an area that has

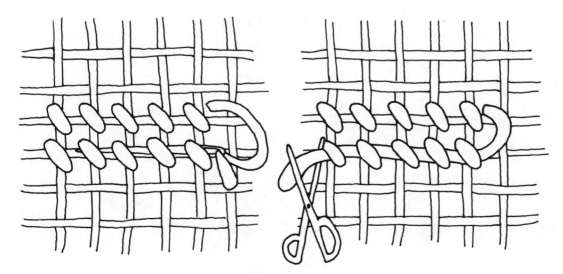

finishing a strand

not previously been worked at all. From this point on, all new strands of wool can be woven in on the back of the design over one stitch and under the next for about an inch. Complete the end of a strand with the same weaving. Weave carefully and evenly to prevent ridges from showing on the front (*see diagram, page 24*). After the strand is woven, look at the final stitch on the front, and if it has been pulled a little too tight, loosen it slightly with your needle so it has the same tension as the surrounding stitches. Cut the little tail off so it will not get caught in succeeding stitches.

CONTINENTAL (OR HORIZONTAL TENT) STITCH

To work the Continental stitch, you complete one row going from right to left. You then turn the canvas upside down and work a row going back. Care must be taken never to work two successive rows in the same direction—in other words, without reversing the canvas. If you do, you will have an unsightly ridge when the work is finished that no amount of blocking, tugging or pulling will remove. The Continental stitch is used for outlining and for small areas where the Diagonal Tent (or Basketweave) stitch cannot be used. Using the

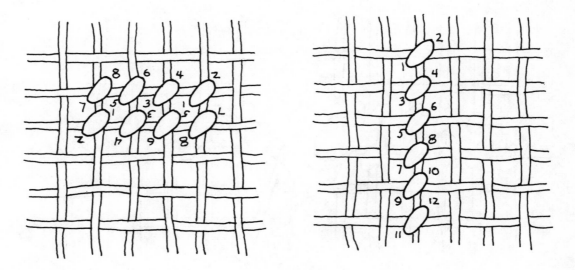

Continental stitch—horizontal and vertical

Continental stitch for large areas often distorts the canvas so badly that numerous blockings will not straighten it and keep it straight.

To work the Continental stitch, bring your needle with the wool from the back to the front of the canvas. Insert it one mesh above and one mesh to the right and, without pulling the wool through, insert the needle through to the front of the canvas one mesh below and two meshes to the left. Pull the yarn through. Again insert the needle one mesh above and one mesh to the right; bring it out one mesh below and two meshes to the left. Pull the yarn through. Continue doing this until the end of the row. To turn, instead of inserting your needle two meshes to the left, insert it one mesh below the last stitch and pull the yarn through. You are now ready to turn the canvas and repeat the same stitch back.

BASKETWEAVE (OR DIAGONAL TENT) STITCH

This stitch has a number of advantages over the Continental stitch, especially for working large areas. It distorts the canvas only slightly if at all, and the need to keep turning your canvas around is eliminated, since you work in a diagonal line from top to bottom and bottom to top. Again, as in the Continental, never work two successive rows in the same direction.

To work the Basketweave stitch, bring your needle from the back of the canvas to the front, at the upper right-hand corner. Insert it one mesh above and one mesh to the right, bringing it out one mesh below and two meshes to the left. Pull the yarn through. Reinsert the needle one mesh above and one mesh to the right, and bring it out two meshes directly below. Pull the yarn through. Reinsert the needle one mesh above and one mesh to the right, bringing it out two meshes below and one mesh to the left. Pull the yarn through. Reinsert the needle one mesh above and one mesh to the right, and bring it out again horizontally two meshes to the left. Pull the yarn through. Reinsert the needle one mesh above and one mesh to the right, and bring it out horizontally two meshes to the left. Pull the yarn through. Reinsert the needle one mesh above and one mesh to the right, and bring it out one mesh below and two meshes to the left. Pull the yarn through. You have now

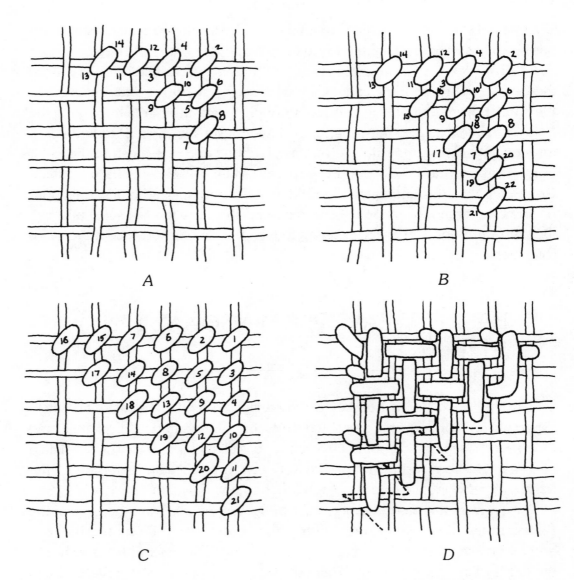

A, B and C—working the Basketweave   D—wrong side of work

established the basic pattern for your stitches (*see above*). Remember that the needle will always be vertical as you work down and horizontal as you work up.

Both of these stitches can be used on the same piece of work, as they look the same on the right side. Instead of trying to work a solid area in the Basketweave stitch directly from the graph, first outline the area with the Continental stitch and then fill in with the Basketweave. Then you will only have to count the stitches once, instead of continually checking the graph to see if each row has the proper number of stitches. Also, if you make a mistake, you will only have to rip a single line of stitches back to the error, rather than row after row.

Here are basic rules and tips for creating beautiful needlepoint:

1) Never leave a knot on the back of needlepoint. It will show on the front even after blocking.

2) When weaving the end of a piece of yarn on the reverse of the design, if at all possible, weave it with the vertical or horizontal stitches, and not on the diagonal.

3) As much as possible, do not end and start new strands of wool over and over close to one another. Otherwise, a ridge may appear on the wrong side and cause a bump on the front. If you see this happening, cut a few strands longer or shorter.

4) If you find you have not reversed your line of stitching, do rip it out, no matter how much you would rather cut your wrists. It will keep you from having that unsightly line I have already mentioned.

5) If you finish a strand of yarn and decide to stop work, either leave the needle tucked into the canvas with the end of the yarn in it, or leave the tail loose on the front of the canvas. You can weave it in when you start working again. Do this as well if you are working with more than one color or at more than one place on your design at the same time. If you stop work in the middle of a row, you can see where you have stopped if you look closely. Nevertheless, it is safer to leave the little unwoven tail hanging loose. It is surprising how easy it is to make a mistake.

6) Always trim the little tails of your finished strand close to the back of your work. Cut them *very* close—in fact, as close as you can without actually slicing your stitching. If you do not, tiny little hairs of the wool will get caught in the next rows of stitches, and if you have changed colors, you will have a subtle shading which will blur edges that should be sharp and give a grayed look to colors that should be clear and bright.

7) Always be sure all your stitches consistently slant in the same direction. If you make a mistake and slant some in an opposite direction, rip them right out.

8) Be sure your wool is covering your canvas. Remember that, while bread that tastes homemade is dreamy, needlepoint with that loving-hands-at-home look is only amateurish.

9) Do not try to take a misplaced stitch out by pushing your threaded needle through to the back or through to the front. Unthread the needle and carefully pick the wool back through the canvas. Too often, if you try to take a stitch out with a threaded needle, you will catch the tiniest bit of wool, the stitch will not come out, and you will be in much worse trouble than you were to begin with.

10) Although you can rip a few stitches and continue using the same piece of yarn, throw the strand away and start a new one if you have extensive ripping. Ripping, for some reason, no matter how carefully it is done, frays the wool far more than working it into the canvas.

11) If you notice that you have split the wool of a previous stitch, unthread your needle and remove the stitch. Do the same if you split a canvas thread. Split stitches look uneven and are the most awful little horrors if you find you have made a mistake that needs ripping.

12) If you must cut stitches in order to remove them, do so with great caution. Use the tips of your sharp scissors and cut gently and slowly. If you feel a resistance, it means the canvas thread is between the blades. If you should cut one strand of canvas, don't panic. Rip the stitches around it carefully, trying not to loosen the meshes surrounding the cut strand. Then pull a strand of canvas from a scrap, lay it over the cut strand and rework your stitches on top of it.

13) Always wash your hands before beginning to work. Do not *ever* read a newspaper and work without washing your hands, and never put your work on top of a newspaper or vice versa. Newsprint transfers insidiously.

14) Always work your design first and your background last.

15) When working small areas of color, such as the violet petals and yellow centers in the rabbit design or spots in the cats or giraffes, you can skip over an area of an inch or so and continue working the same color without anchoring and cutting your yarn. If the area skipped over has already been worked, weave your yarn through on the back as though completing a strand to the point where you will begin stitching again. If it has not been worked, succeeding stitches will cover the loose thread on the back. Do not try to skip over large areas.

16) After you have ripped a mistake, whether by picking the stitches out or cutting them, carefully remove all the bits of fuzz that are left clinging to

the canvas before beginning to replace them. This is particularly important if you are changing colors.

17) As you work stitch after stitch, the strand of yarn will become twisted. Rolling the needle between your fingers a half-turn before each stitch will keep the strand fairly even. Still, you should drop the needle at frequent intervals and let it unwind.

18) Do not store leftover wool in a closed plastic bag or any airtight place. Wool is a natural fiber and needs to breathe. Without air it becomes matted. I have found that empty coffee cans without tops are marvelous for keeping bits and pieces of leftover wool. I keep all shades of a single color in one can with a little snip of the wool taped to the side. Larger amounts of wool can be draped over a coat hanger with a loose plastic bag, open at the bottom, over it to protect it from dust. The wool stays clean and unmatted, and you can see at a glance the colors you have.

19) Always keep in mind that wool appears somewhat darker when stitched on the canvas than it does loose. So if you need to match a color, be sure to take some loose strands to the shop and not just the stitched canvas.

20) There will be times when you have stitched a large area only to realize you have one stitch or more that needs changing. This can be repaired without ripping, provided it is only a matter of very few stitches. Anchor your wool in back as though you were doing a large area, and stitch over the mistake, pulling the wool tight and working it a little with the needle to make sure it covers. Then anchor the wool in back as usual. This works with dark over light wool, but the reverse does not work as well. There is another method, which is really outright cheating and should not become a habit but which can be used if you have to rip a large area to change one or two stitches. With your fine-pointed indelible marker or a brush with paint on a fine tip, simply paint the exact color over the errant stitch. Be very careful. Don't make it a habit!

Chapter Three

The Use of Color

COLOR HAS BEEN USED for decorative purposes since prehistoric times. It can contribute to a sense of well-being, or it can jangle the nerves, and certain combinations can actually cause pain in the eyes. When working with color, choose the ones that appeal to you and soothe you. You must live with them. Do not be bound by what fashion says is correct only because it is fashionable.

Primary colors are red, yellow and blue. They exist. They cannot be achieved by mixing other colors. Secondary colors are orange, green and violet, and all of these are made by the mixture of two primary colors. For example, a mixture of red and yellow produces orange; yellow and blue produce green; blue and red produce violet. Usually two secondary colors combine better with one primary color than two primaries with one secondary. There are also tertiary colors. Red-orange is between red and orange; orange-yellow is between orange and yellow; yellow-green is between yellow and green and so on. On a color wheel, each color is opposite to its complement (*see illustration*).

Warm colors are red, yellow and orange. Cool colors are green, blue and violet. However a yellow-green or a red-violet might appear to be neutral depending on the colors surrounding it. White and all light colors repeal heat; black and all dark colors absorb heat. Light colors advance and dark colors recede.

Color plus white produces tint. Color plus black produces shade. True colors are hues. Tones are lightness or darkness. Color mixed with its complement produces gray. The determination of whether colors work together depends entirely on the tints, shades, hues and tones of the various colors used. Colors that have the same tonal value used in the same amounts next to each other will often blend so as to seem one color, but a harmonious color scheme can be achieved by the use of colors that are closely related but different in tint and shade.

Not too long ago, fashion decreed that using certain colors together was downright gauche. Some examples are blue and green, orange and pink, blue and brown. Rigid rules for what colors went with what were strictly observed both in decoration and in wearing apparel. More recently all bars to color use have fallen and we know from observing nature that any color can be used with any other. But nature has judiciously used the brilliant primary colors as exclamation points. A large field of green will be spotted with bright yellow

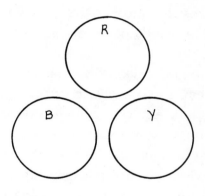

primary colors

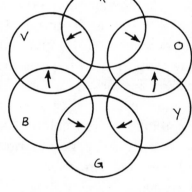

primary and secondary colors

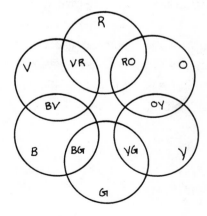

intermediate colors

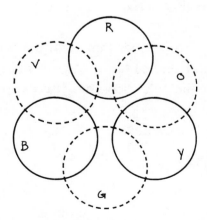

complementary colors

dandelions and goldenrod; a dark-green holly tree has sparkling red berries; the green berries of summer bittersweet burst open in the fall with a glowing splash of red and yellow against a background of leaves turning rust and brown. Even the flaming colors of leaves turning color with the approach of winter last only a short time, as though nature had decided to end a season with one brilliant accent color.

One important thing to remember is that, except for the white of true albinos or snow, there is no pure white and no absolute black in nature. Animal fur or bird feathers that seem completely black will show a tinge of brown, red or blue in strong sunlight. The melanistic, or black, phases of the leopard and jaguar, for example—both of which are born in the same litters with spotted brothers and sisters—will show definite color in bright light. Most fine needle-point yarns come in many blacks and whites that are not the pure form. In Eva's designs it is generally best to use these slightly off colors, as both pure black and white will look unnatural and startling.

In needlepoint, the more shading used from light to dark in any single color, the more natural the design will appear. Eva's ability to design animals realistically using no more than four shades of any one color is due to her complete understanding of their natural form. She uses simple, basic lines in her interpretations. The colors given for her designs are deliberately realistic, but you need not be bound by these colors. A blue background can be changed, without losing its realistic look, to pale green or mustard yellow or the pink of an evening sky, if that will make the finished work more adaptable to your color scheme. Such artistic fancy explains why the actual finished projects in this book sometimes differ from the corresponding graphs and their color keys.

Remember that color plays an important role in every part of modern life, and one of its most personal uses is in the home. If you have a mono-chromatic color scheme, you can make Eva's designs less realistic and more suited to your decoration by changing all the colors. You will still retain realism in the line of the animals.

ON THE GRAPHS, every tenth line, both horizontal and vertical, is a heavy line. Always mark these lines on your canvas to match the graphs before beginning to work. Each square within these heavy lines contains 100 small squares, each square representing one stitch. The heavy lines are a reference point for the stitches within them and also in relation to the design as a whole. After cutting your canvas to size and binding the edges, fold it in half, and in half again, once vertically and once horizontally. Mark the point in the center where the two folds meet. This mark is shown on the graph as an X. Draw a very light line radiating to the four sides from this point. Mark the top of your canvas. Count the small squares from the center to the top of the graph. Count an equal number of canvas meshes and draw a horizontal line across the canvas. Do the same at the bottom and sides. This will give the outline for the design. (*See illustration showing marked canvas.*) Then lightly draw the heavy lines on your canvas exactly as they appear on the graph.

The size of the finished piece in the individual designs can be changed, if you choose, by simply changing the gauge of the canvas.

If you have access to a photography shop or studio, you may wish to have the graphs photostated to a larger size. The photographic method of enlarging a design is both inexpensive, and convenient if you do needlework when you travel. You can take the photostat instead of the book and lighten your load. Do not forget to include the color keys to the graph symbols. If you find the graph symbols confusing, it might help to lightly color in the graph.

If you prefer to draw and paint the design

Chapter Four

Twenty Designs with Graph Patterns

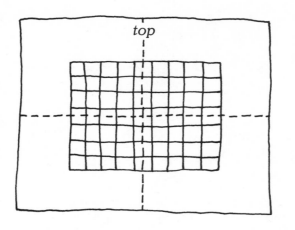

marked canvas

on canvas rather than work directly from the graph, have the design photostated to the size you want and trace it on your canvas, using the same procedure as you would for an original design (*see chapter 5*).

In a geometric design, if you make one wrong stitch, it will throw the entire design off. With Eva's flowing, realistic designs, you need not follow exactly stitch for stitch. You can add or subtract stitches or even misplace a stitch; your design will still have a beautiful, natural look. You can also isolate elements of certain compositions—such as the frog in "Jaguar Cub with Frog," one of the rabbits, or zebras—and work them on canvas as separate, original designs.

Unless you have had experience with blocking and finishing needlepoint pillows, it is best to take your work to a professional.

Except where indicated, all the designs in this book were stitched with Paternayan wool and the numbers and colors listed refer to their color chart.

THE CAT FAMILY

Cats are divided into two distinct classes; the roarers and the purrers. The cats that roar are the lion, tiger, jaguar, leopard and snow leopard. The rest can only purr or growl, though to an untrained ear others may seem to roar. All have a connection between the larynx and skull by means of small bones called hyoid bones. In the large cats, the hyoid bones are separated by an elastic ligament, which gives them the sounding board for a full-throated, ground-shaking roar. In the wild, a lion's roar can be heard for several miles. The five roaring cats are in a genus called *Panthera*; all others are *Felis*.

All cats hiss or spit when frightened or angry. Cats purr, not only when they are happy, as most people think, but also when in pain, although there is a distinct difference in the type of purr. Some wild cats have a birdlike chirp and some have a shrill, high-pitched scream.

Cats' eyes are particularly adapted to seeing in dim light and, in fact, most cats are nocturnal hunters. No animal can see in absolute darkness.

Cats, unless miserably unhappy, are immaculate animals. They will bathe not only themselves but also their friends. Their tongues are coated with little thorny projections, which have been adapted to help lick flesh from a carcass. Our pet cat likes to wash my husband's hair and does it with such determination that I've always been afraid that one day he will wash him bald.

All cats have retractable claws, with the exception of the cheetah, which, in any case, is in a related genus by itself.

The Lion Pride

Like most of the larger animals, the lion has steadily retreated before the advance of man. Some species of lion became extinct in the last century, and the last Indian lions in the Gir Forest, although legally protected, are in serious danger due to human encroachment with tens of thousands of domestic animals on their territory. However, the large herds of hoofed animals both inside and outside of the national parks of Africa provide a healthy diet for African lions, and they are holding their own there. Also, unlike many of the other wild cats, they breed prolifically in captivity.

Apart from mating and raising their young, cats are solitary animals and are perfectly content to ignore others of their kind. Not so the unique lion. Lions live in family groups called prides, containing anywhere from three to twenty or more members. Both males and females are tolerant of the infant lions, allowing them the liberty of crawling on them, biting their tails, swatting their faces and, in general, acting exactly like all babies everywhere.

The title "King of Beasts" belongs to the lion probably because of his noble stature and earth-shaking roar and not because of his personality, which, although courageous, is decidedly languorous. Lions are not normally aggressive, but from time to time a fierce battle will be waged between them. Most of these fights can be attributed to the mating season, and they rarely result in death.

Only the male has a mane, which starts growing when the lion is about three years old. Lion cubs are born with thick, spotted coats of fur. The spots gradually disappear as the lion grows older.

Eva's brush captures the traits of magnificent courage, nobility and serenity of all lions everywhere.

Male and Female Lion Heads

This design has 226 stitches by 226 stitches at its widest points. The original was stitched on 14-gauge mono canvas. The finished pillow measures 16 inches in circumference.

Cut a piece of canvas 20 inches square. Bind the edges. Mark the center stitch. Copy the heavy graph lines lightly on your canvas and outline the square. Mark the canvas top. Do not try to draw the circle on canvas. Follow the graph lines for this.

The nine suggested colors as they appear in the original are:

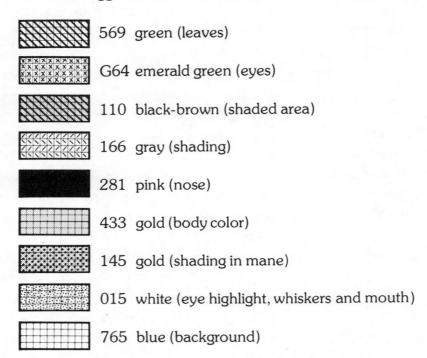

569 green (leaves)

G64 emerald green (eyes)

110 black-brown (shaded area)

166 gray (shading)

281 pink (nose)

433 gold (body color)

145 gold (shading in mane)

015 white (eye highlight, whiskers and mouth)

765 blue (background)

Twenty
Designs
with Graph
Patterns

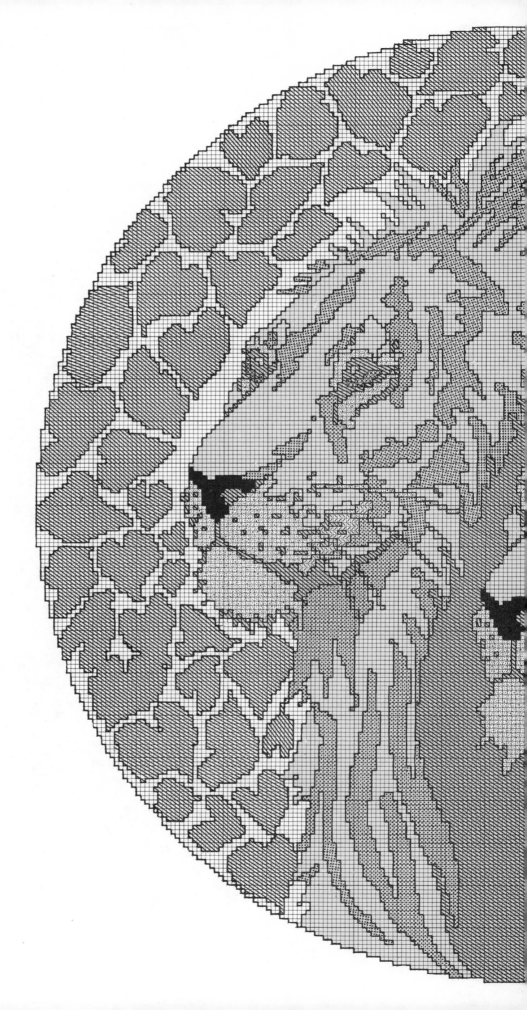

Lion Cub in Octagonal Border

This design has 244 stitches by 210 stitches at the two widest points. The original was stitched on 14-gauge mono canvas. The finished pillow measures 17½ inches by 15 inches.

Cut a piece of canvas 21½ inches by 19 inches. Bind the edges. Mark the center stitch. Draw the heavy graph lines lightly on your canvas. Do not try to draw the slanting sides of the octagon. Follow the graph for those lines. Mark the canvas top.

The fifteen suggested colors as they appear in the original are:

Center colors:

050 black (eye, tail and claws)

015 white (lion)

G64 emerald green (eye)

281 pink (nose)

445 gold (lion body color)

462 gold-brown (lion shading)

166 light gray (shading in ears and paws)

164 gray (shading in ears)

411 brown (whiskers and shading on lion)

143 beige (background)

Border:

228 violet (blossoms and treetrunks)

631 lavender (leaves and blossoms)

385 dark gray-blue (treetrunk and treetops)

395 light gray-blue (leaves and treetops)

011 white (border background)

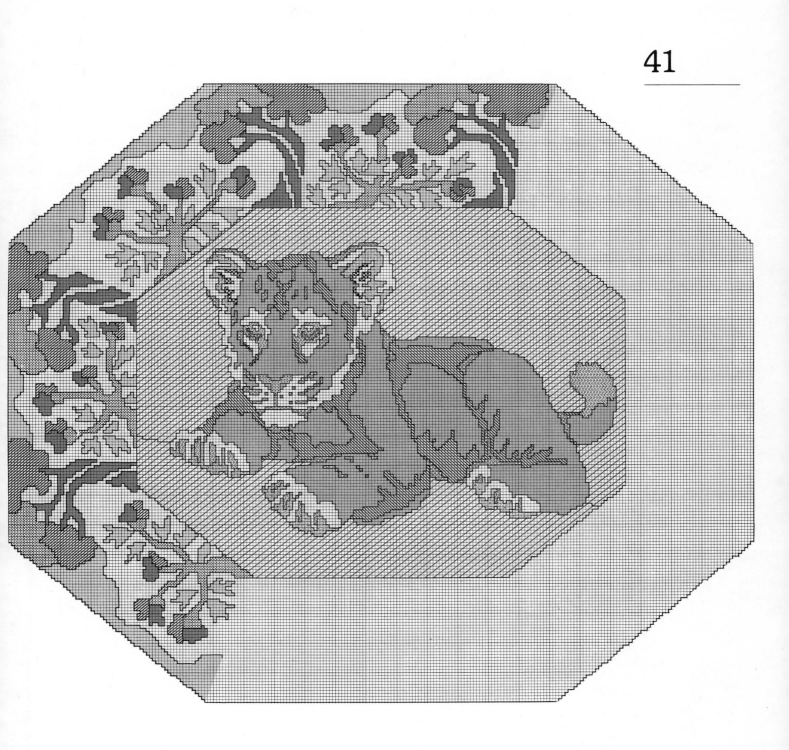

Twenty
Designs
with Graph
Patterns

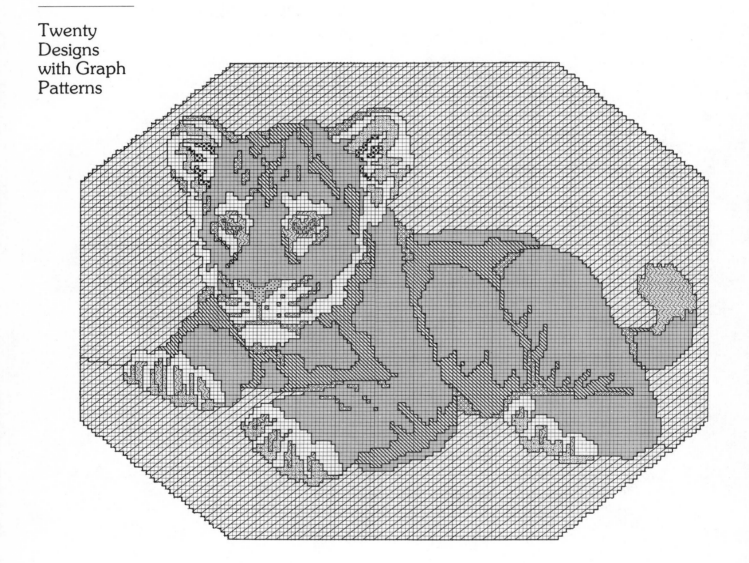

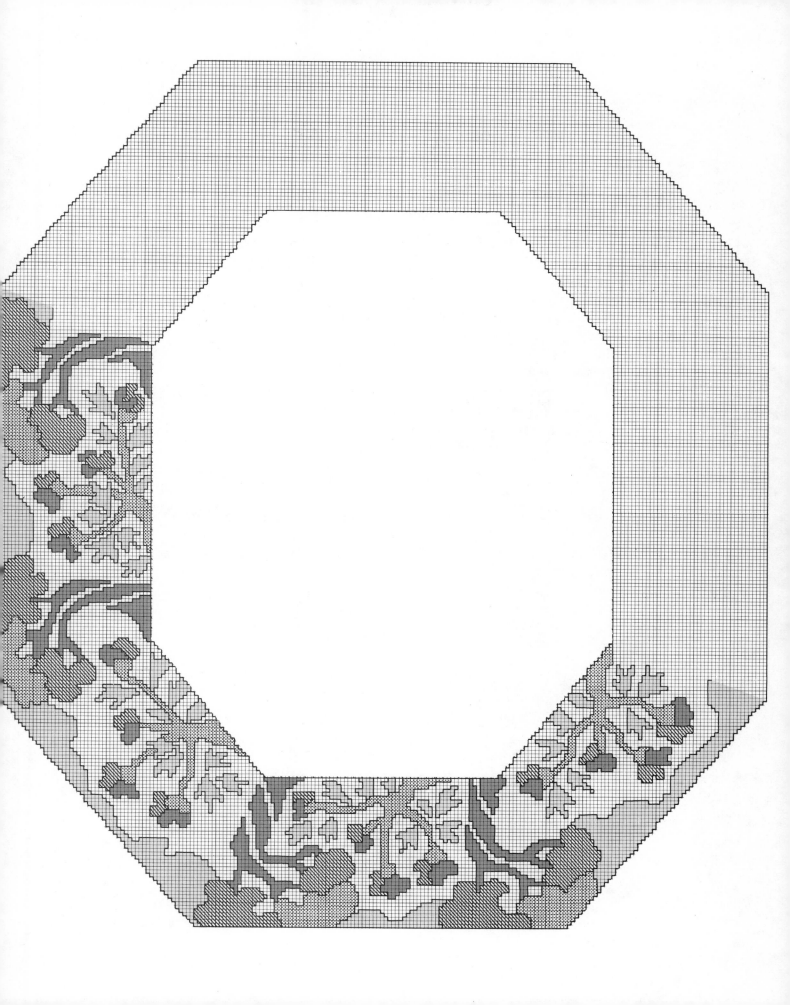

Resting Male Lion

This design has 192 by 247 stitches. The original was stitched on 14-gauge mono canvas. The finished piece will measure 13½ inches by 17½ inches.

Cut a piece of canvas 17¾ inches by 21½ inches. Bind the edges. Mark the center stitch. Draw the heavy graph lines lightly on your canvas and outline the rectangle. Mark the canvas top.

The twelve suggested colors are:

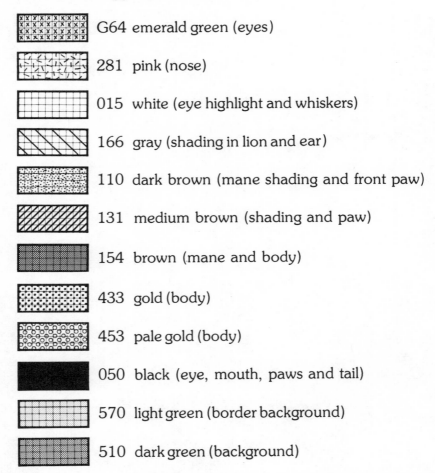

G64 emerald green (eyes)

281 pink (nose)

015 white (eye highlight and whiskers)

166 gray (shading in lion and ear)

110 dark brown (mane shading and front paw)

131 medium brown (shading and paw)

154 brown (mane and body)

433 gold (body)

453 pale gold (body)

050 black (eye, mouth, paws and tail)

570 light green (border background)

510 dark green (background)

This design was intended as a companion piece for the Resting Tiger on page 50. The background colors can be the same or contrasting, and either pillow would be equally effective used alone. Instead of showing the finished pillow, we have shown how the pillow looks as it is being worked directly from the graph.

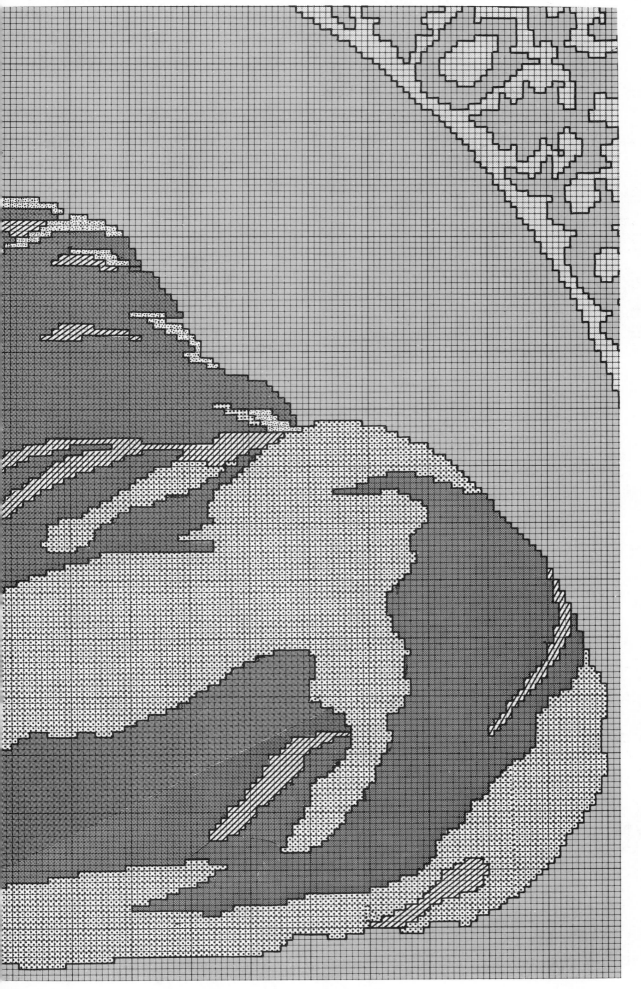

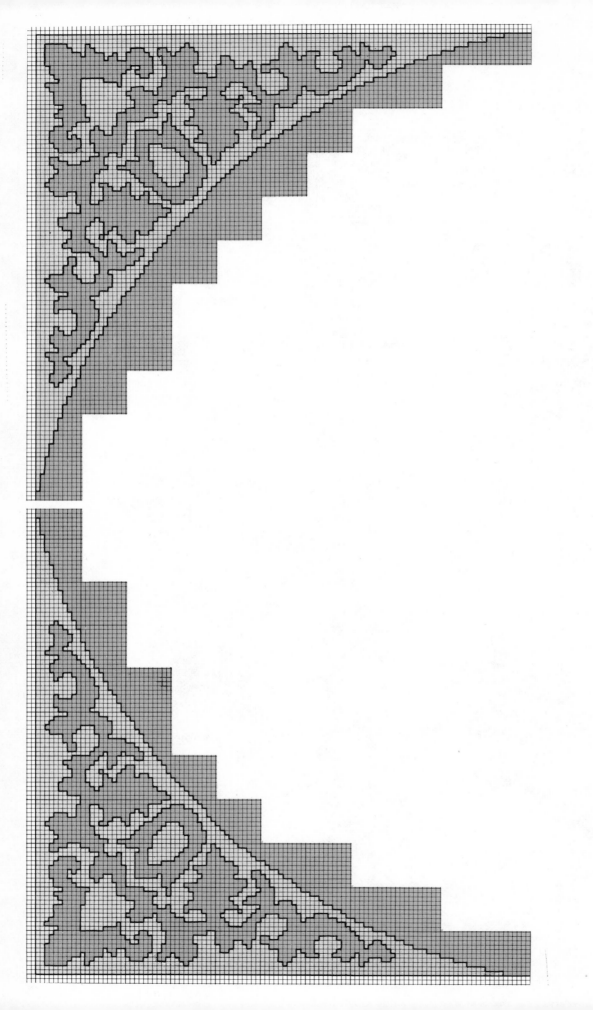

Unfortunately, the association between man and tiger, the largest of the great cats, has been mainly on a kill-or-be-killed basis. Tigers are purely Asiatic, and there are at present no more than 2,500 of all races of tiger roaming free. It is a sad fact that in a few years there will almost surely be none. There are twice as many Siberian tigers in zoos as there are in the wild and, to the zoos' everlasting credit, most of these were zoo-born, not captured. There are probably more tiger skins on floors in New York City, hanging in closets and safely tucked in cold storage rooms than there are tigers left in the wild. If this magnificent beast is to survive at all, it will have to be in the better zoos, which are making valiant efforts to keep the species from extinction.

Where man has encroached on the tigers' territory in countries such as India with large, rural communities, it is true that people have occasionally been killed by individual tigers. When this happened, great hunts were organized and innocent as well as guilty tigers were slaughtered. Only fairly recently have we been made aware that when a large cat turns man-killer, it is very likely an old or sick animal, pressed by hunger, that has trouble catching the swift prey of his usual diet and has found weak, slow-moving man easier to deal with. Every wild cat would much prefer to have no contact with man at all.

Many cats, from the small house cat to the large jaguar have a melanistic or black phase, but there has never been a proven case of a black tiger. There are, however, white tigers, called "sports." In 1951 the Maharajah of Rewa managed to capture a male white tiger alive and unharmed. He named him Mohan and began a breeding colony. Since then, many zoos have obtained one or more of Mohan's descendants and have gone on to breed their own. These beautiful beasts are white with charcoal and silver-gray stripes, pink pads on their feet, pink noses and ice-blue eyes. Therefore, if you want to change the color of the tigers Eva has drawn, you will be perfectly correct in using these colors instead of the normal tiger colors of yellow, gold, white and black.

Resting Tiger

This design has 247 stitches by 192 stitches. The original was stitched on 14-gauge mono canvas. The finished pillow measures 17½ inches by 13¾ inches.

Cut a piece of canvas 21½ inches by 17¾ inches. Bind the edges. Mark the center stitch. Draw the heavy graph lines on your canvas lightly and outline the rectangle. Mark the canvas top.

The twelve suggested colors as they appear in the original are:

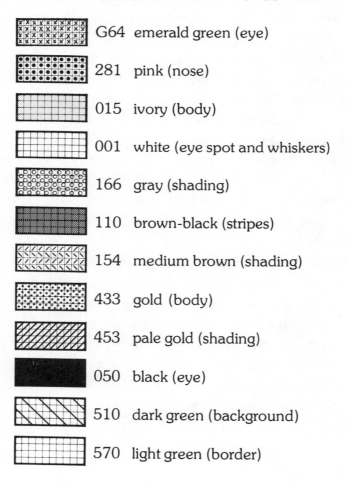

G64   emerald green (eye)

281   pink (nose)

015   ivory (body)

001   white (eye spot and whiskers)

166   gray (shading)

110   brown-black (stripes)

154   medium brown (shading)

433   gold (body)

453   pale gold (shading)

050   black (eye)

510   dark green (background)

570   light green (border)

This design was intended as a companion piece for the Resting Male Lion on page 44. The background colors can be the same or contrasting; either pillow would be equally effective used alone.

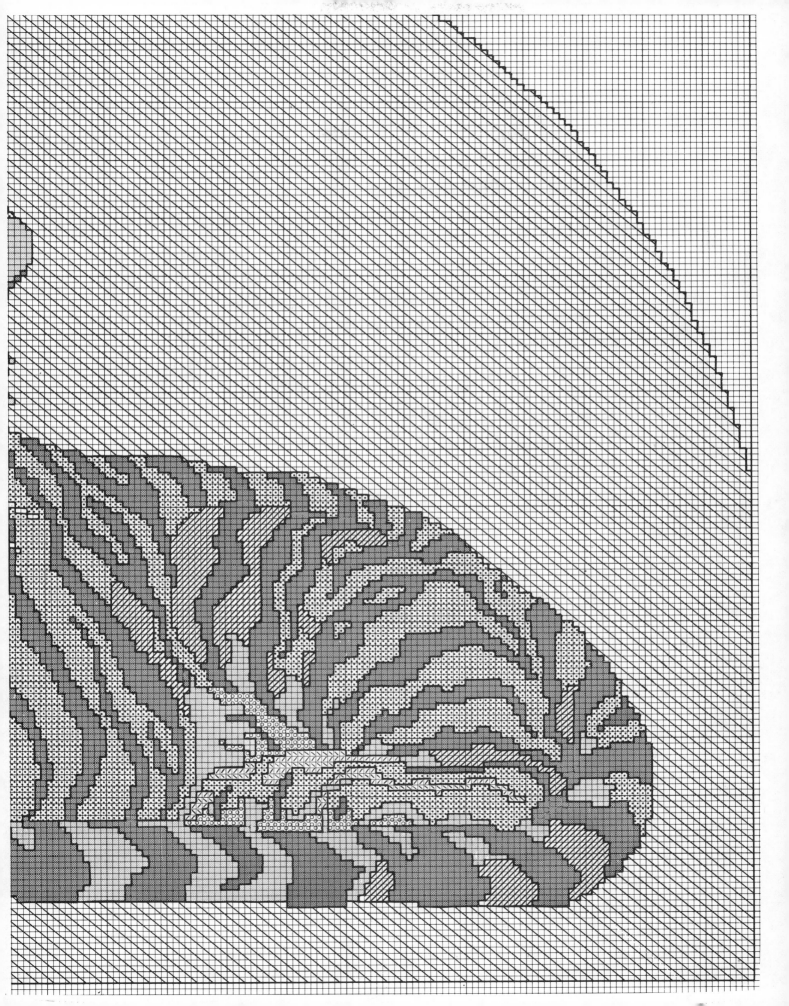

Tiger Cub with Bee

This design has 220 stitches by 220 stitches. The original was stitched on 14-gauge mono canvas. The finished pillow measures 15¾ inches at its widest points.

Cut a piece of canvas 19¾ inches square. Bind the edges. Mark the center stitch. Draw the heavy graph lines on your canvas lightly and outline the square. Mark the canvas top.

The twelve suggested colors as they appear in the original are:

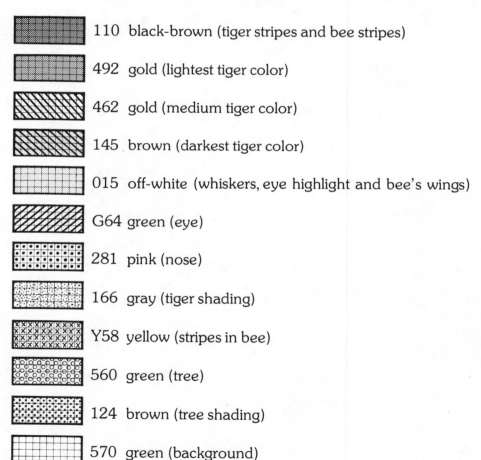

110 black-brown (tiger stripes and bee stripes)

492 gold (lightest tiger color)

462 gold (medium tiger color)

145 brown (darkest tiger color)

015 off-white (whiskers, eye highlight and bee's wings)

G64 green (eye)

281 pink (nose)

166 gray (tiger shading)

Y58 yellow (stripes in bee)

560 green (tree)

124 brown (tree shading)

570 green (background)

The Jaguar

The jaguar is the only one of the roaring cats to inhabit the New World. Though considerably larger than the leopard, it can be considered the leopard's counterpart in America, and the two may have descended from a common ancestor.

Its fur pattern differs somewhat from the leopard's. The jaguar has black spots arranged in rosettes of four or five spots with dark centers, which become solid spots on the flanks, back and legs. The color varies from pale yellow to tawny or the melanistic phase of all black. Even on black jaguars, however, the spots are still visible. Both black and spotted young are born in the same litter.

Jaguars have been hunted mercilessly for their exquisite pelts, but fortunately now they have been placed on the Endangered Species list of the United States. Some South American states, as well, have banned hunting them for either trophies or fur, and if certain areas are left as wilderness, there is hope this largest American cat will survive.

Like their larger cousins, the tigers, jaguars love to swim and play in water. Usually two to four cubs are born to a litter, and the young will stay with the mother for about two years until they, in turn, are adult and ready to start their own families.

Jaguar Cub with Frog

This design has 225 stitches by 220 stitches. Instead of showing the finished needlepoint, we have shown how the canvas looks if the design is painted before being graphed. If you use 14-gauge mono canvas to follow the graph, the finished work will measure 16 inches by 15¾ inches.

Cut a piece of canvas 20 inches by 19¾ inches. Bind the edges. Mark the center stitch. Copy the heavy graph lines lightly on your canvas and outline the square. Mark the canvas top.

The fourteen suggested colors as they appear in the original painting are:

G64   emerald green (eyes and grass)

001   white (whiskers)

015   ivory (around eyes, ears, paws and neck)

166   gray (shading)

110   brown-black (spots)

433   gold (shading)

453   pale gold (shading)

131   medium brown (shading)

242   red (frog)

Y52   yellow (frog)

740   blue (frog body and inner eye)

754   blue (frog eye and lower background)

578   blue (upper background)

G54   green (grass)

Cheetah

Although cheetahs are considered relatives of the cat family, they have certain characteristics that are more canine than feline. They do not climb trees and do not have sharp, sheathed, completely retractable claws.

Cheetahs are the fastest land animals on earth. In the wild, however, even their great speed does not always guarantee them a successful kill, as they cannot sustain the speed for long distances. For this reason, they can only survive where there is an abundance of prey animals. They are generally considered to be the most reliable of the big cats in captivity and, in fact, have been trained for hunting from earliest times.

Because of the beauty of the cheetahs' fur, they have suffered great attrition through hunting. As a result of hunting and the destruction of their habitat, cheetahs have declined rapidly throughout most of their range, disappeared entirely in many areas of Africa and are considered extinct in India. They are now on the Endangered Species list, and it is hoped that this, plus the fact that it is becoming less and less popular to wear furs made from wild cats, will keep cheetahs in the wild from disappearing completely.

Cheetah with Cub

This design has 222 stitches by 188 stitches. The original should be stitched on 14-gauge mono canvas. We have shown it as it appears painted on the canvas from which the graph was made. The finished piece measures 15¾ inches by 13½ inches.

Cut a piece of canvas 19¾ inches by 17¾ inches. Bind the edges. Mark the center stitch. Copy the heavy graph lines lightly on your canvas and outline the rectangle. Mark the canvas top.

The twelve colors as they appear in the original are:

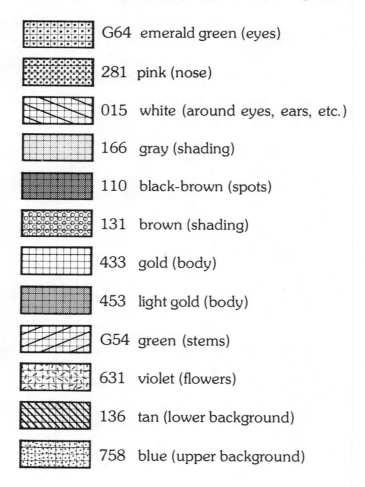

G64   emerald green (eyes)

281   pink (nose)

015   white (around eyes, ears, etc.)

166   gray (shading)

110   black-brown (spots)

131   brown (shading)

433   gold (body)

453   light gold (body)

G54   green (stems)

631   violet (flowers)

136   tan (lower background)

758   blue (upper background)

Page 44

Page 62

Page 58

Page 66

Page 54

Page 74

Page 70

Page 36

Page 40

Page 82

Page 86

Page 90

Page 78

Page 50

Page 118

Page 114

Page 102

Page 108

Page 94

Page 98

AFRICAN ELEPHANT

The most striking characteristics of elephants are their size and weight, both of which are exceeded only by the larger whales. African elephants differ from Indian elephants in a number of ways, of which the most visible are these: (1) their size is usually greater, (2) their ears are enormous as compared with the Indians', (3) their heads are larger and more elegant and (4) their tusks are longer and heavier.

At one time, these giants of the animal kingdom were found throughout Africa, but due to the pressures of the ivory hunters in the last part of the nineteenth century and the early part of the twentieth century, as well as the encroachment of civilization on their range, they are now confined almost entirely within the tropical area and much of their range there has been reduced to national parks. Elephants are vegetarians, and, for all practical purposes, have no enemy except man, although infrequently a lion or other carnivore will try, sometimes successfully, to grab a helpless infant. These babies are guarded with much care and devotion by the older elephants. When danger threatens, a large group of females will completely surround the infants to protect them from harm. The matriarch, or herd leader, will make furious, noisy charges toward the source of danger, but the charges are seldom in earnest and, eventually, if left alone, the whole group will move thunderously away.

The African elephant is a majestic, nonaggressive, noble animal, and it is this species and this nobility Eva has captured in her design.

African Elephant with Baby

This design has 208 stitches by 222 stitches. The original was stitched on 14-gauge mono canvas. The finished pillow measures 14¾ inches by 15¾ inches.

Cut a piece of canvas 18¾ inches by 19¾ inches. Bind the edges. Mark the center stitch. Draw the heavy graph lines lightly on your canvas and outline the square. Mark the canvas top.

The nine suggested colors as they appear in the original are:

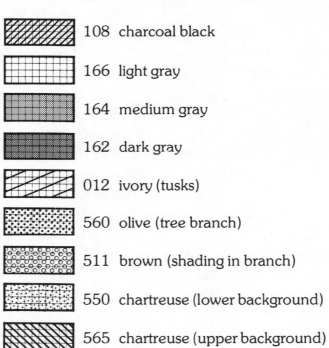

108 charcoal black

166 light gray

164 medium gray

162 dark gray

012 ivory (tusks)

560 olive (tree branch)

511 brown (shading in branch)

550 chartreuse (lower background)

565 chartreuse (upper background)

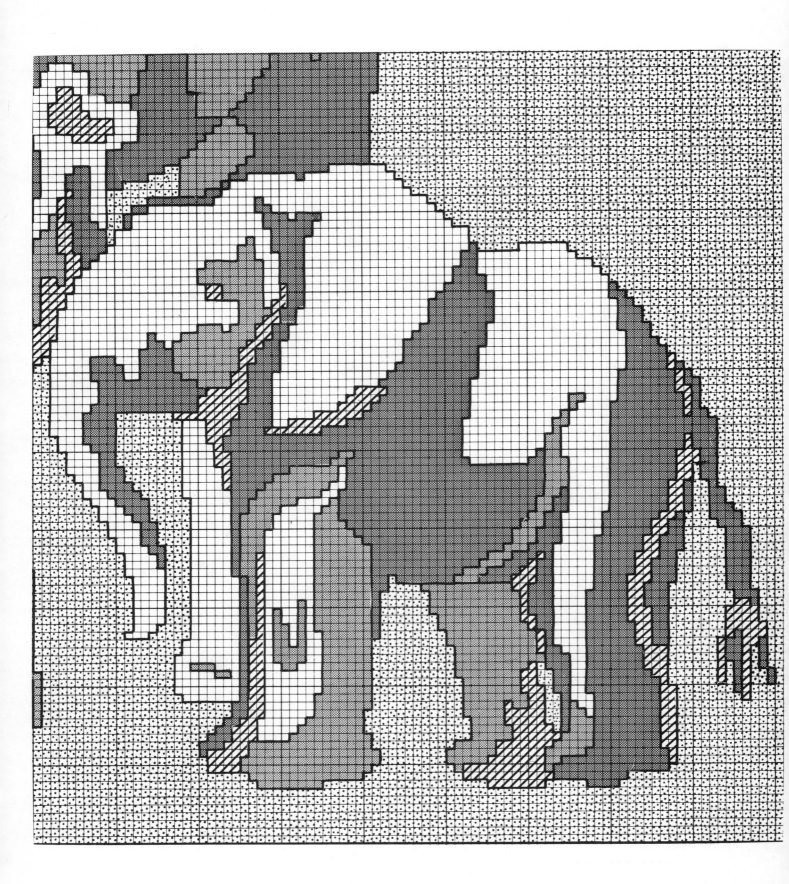

THE ZEBRA

There are tens of thousands of zebras in great herds in Africa and many hundreds more in the world's zoos, where they breed easily. Still this is an enormous reduction in numbers from the countless animals that once roamed the plains. Several kinds have been wiped out entirely, and so, even though most races appear to be in no danger, care must be taken to keep the herds in numbers that will assure their survival.

The zebra is one of the main sources of food for lions. Zebras appear to notice when lions are hungry and hunting or when they are satiated and sleepy. They will graze unconcernedly with a sleeping pride of lions nearby but will become nervous and ready for a moment's stampeding flight when lions are on the prowl.

It would appear that the dramatic striping of zebras would make them stand out against the tawny grasses of the plains where they live. In fact, we now know that because the carnivores, whose prey they are, do not see color, the stripes are a perfect form of protective coloration.

Pair of Zebras

This design has 180 stitches by 180 stitches. The original was stitched on 14-gauge mono canvas. The finished pillow measures 13 inches by 13 inches.

Cut a piece of canvas 17 inches square. Bind the edges. Mark the center stitch. Draw the heavy graph lines lightly on your canvas and outline the square. Mark the canvas top.

The six suggested colors as they appear in the original are:

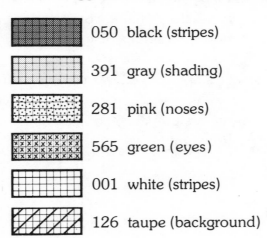

050 black (stripes)

391 gray (shading)

281 pink (noses)

565 green (eyes)

001 white (stripes)

126 taupe (background)

GIRAFFES

Giraffes are native only to Africa. They are the tallest living animals attaining a height of eighteen feet, almost as tall as a two-story building. Early Egyptians thought the giraffe's height enabled him to see into the future. Although they can't see quite that far, their eyes are exceptionally large, prominent and lustrous and command a wide field of vision. They can see and distinguish anything that moves at an approximate distance of three hundred yards. They have two straight protuberances resembling horns, about eight inches long, covered with hair and tufted at the ends. Giraffes run rapidly, even faster than horses, but they cannot swim.

Contrary to many tales, they are not mute but use their low, gentle-sounding voices infrequently. Like cows, they are cud chewers; their favorite food is the tall, thorny acacia tree, and on savannas where it is plentiful so are giraffes.

Giraffe babies are six feet tall and weigh about 160 pounds at birth; only one is born at a time. Except for an occasional lion that will try to make off with an infant, and man, they have no natural enemies. Rarely will even lions try to best an adult giraffe, because with its long, powerful legs and heavy hoofs it can deliver very punishing kicks. In disposition, they are mild and inoffensive and will usually seek safety, if danger threatens, by immediate flight. They are no longer in much danger from poachers, but there are hunters with guns, land to cultivate with machines, and hungry people to feed with its produce—so their future in the wild, as with all large animals, is in need of strict protection.

Two Giraffes with Acacia

This design has 210 stitches by 218 stitches. The original was stitched on 14-gauge mono canvas. The finished pillow measures 15 inches by 15½ inches.

Cut a piece of canvas 19 inches by 19½ inches. Bind the edges. Mark the center stitch. Draw the heavy graph lines lightly on your canvas and outline the square. Mark the canvas top.

The nine suggested colors as they appear in the original are:

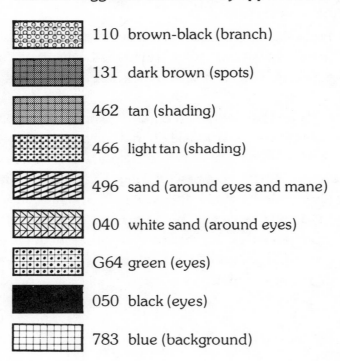

110 brown-black (branch)

131 dark brown (spots)

462 tan (shading)

466 light tan (shading)

496 sand (around eyes and mane)

040 white sand (around eyes)

G64 green (eyes)

050 black (eyes)

783 blue (background)

MONKEY

Monkeys and apes are primates and of all the animals are nearest to man in appearance. The level of intelligence of all monkeys is great. Indeed, their most outstanding characteristic is the development of certain areas of the brain, which are most pronounced in man.

There are both Old World and New World monkeys. All have tails, unlike apes, which do not. No Old World monkeys have prehensile tails, and only some New World monkeys do. The prehensile tail is useful as an additional hand. The largest monkey is the mandrill of equatorial West Africa; the smallest is the pygmy marmoset of South America.

Generally monkeys have only one baby at a time, but as with man, there are exceptions; marmosets frequently have twins. Infant monkeys cling to the fur on the stomach or back of both the mother and the father. In fact, marmoset fathers assume most of the care of the babies, only giving them to the mother to nurse.

Monkeys' fur varies from soft and smooth to harsh and wiry. Some have glorious topknots, crests and collars of fur, and some are more brilliantly colored than any other mammal.

In the wild, monkeys live chiefly in forests in groups of varying sizes, hunting, eating, sleeping together and grooming one another incessantly. Their food consists mostly of fruit and other vegetable substances.

No wild animal makes a good pet, and, in spite of their many resemblances to man, monkeys are no exception. Except in zoos, where their presence is necessary for education and, in some cases, preservation, monkeys and apes should be left alone to enjoy their free-swinging existence.

Monkey Mother and Infant

This design has 190 stitches by 200 stitches. The original was stitched on 14-gauge mono canvas. The finished piece measures 13½ inches by 14¼ inches.

Cut a piece of canvas 17½ inches by 18¼ inches. Bind the edges. Mark the center stitch. Draw the heavy graph lines on your canvas and outline the square. Mark the canvas top.

The eleven suggested colors as they appear in the original are:

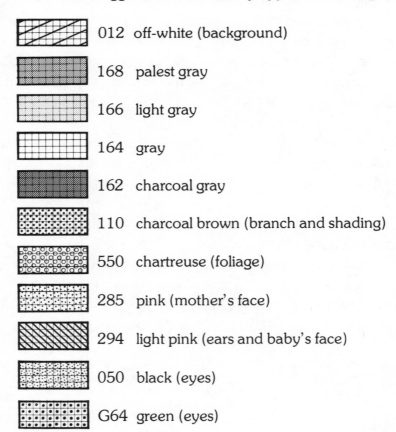

012 off-white (background)

168 palest gray

166 light gray

164 gray

162 charcoal gray

110 charcoal brown (branch and shading)

550 chartreuse (foliage)

285 pink (mother's face)

294 light pink (ears and baby's face)

050 black (eyes)

G64 green (eyes)

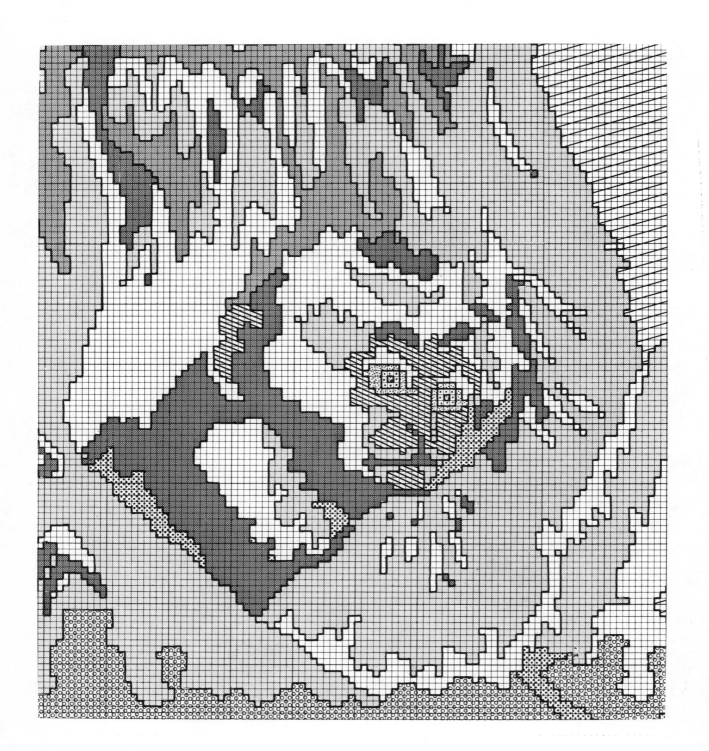

RABBITS

Most people think of rabbits as rodents. They are not. They are in a separate group called lagomorphs. Rodents will eat almost anything, including the wallpaper and the wall. Rabbits are strict vegetarians. Rabbits and hares are not the same animal, even though the words have become almost synonymous. The beautiful so-called snowshoe rabbit of the Arctic, which changes its coat from a summer grayish brown to winter white as a protective device, is in reality a hare.

The wild cottontail cannot be tamed to be a pet even when captured very young, but domestic rabbits are gentle, cuddly, affectionate and very little trouble. All rabbits are timid creatures and are defenseless against predators, but they have acute senses of hearing and smell and often avoid danger by darting into their burrows. They are hunted by man for their fur, as food and as pests, and their survival is testimony to their legendary breeding habits. The young of rabbits are born naked, blind and helpless in a fur-lined nest that the mother has prepared for them, and they will stay there until they are able to forage for themselves in the evening, when rabbits are most active.

The fur of domestic rabbits is varied and colorful. Some are solid color, some have mixed colors, and some have distinctive patterns in shades of reds, oranges, browns, blues and the pure white albino with pink eyes. Eva's design of wild rabbits can be altered to fit almost any color scheme and still remain true to nature.

Two Rabbits with Violets

This design has 200 stitches by 203 stitches. The original was stitched on 14-gauge mono canvas. The finished pillow measures 14¼ inches by 14½ inches.

Cut a piece of canvas 18¼ inches by 18½ inches. Bind the edges. Mark the center stitch. Draw the heavy graph lines lightly on your canvas and outline the square. Mark the canvas top.

The eleven suggested colors as they appear in the original are:

153 off-white (whiskers, eye highlights, around eyes, <u>under</u> nose of rabbit at right)

143 light beige

133 medium beige

123 dark beige

R10 red (eye)

229 violet (flowers)

G64 light green (foliage)

G54 dark green (foliage)

446 yellow (flower centers)

050 black (eyes)

323 blue (background)

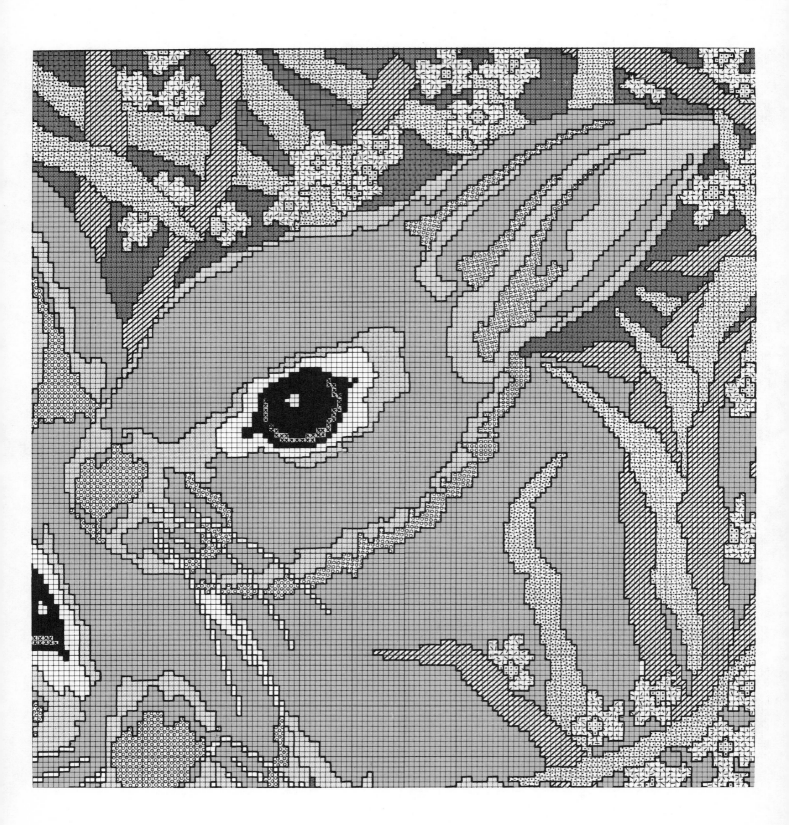

OWLS

Owls are among the most misunderstood of birds, both for good and ill. They are represented in rhyme and story as intelligent and benevolent on one hand and malevolent and destructive on the other. They are portrayed as wise and gentle, cruel and cunning. In reality, they have no more of any of these qualities than any other bird of prey. They are complicated birds possessed by a combination of characteristics that makes their role necessary in the wildlife community. They are very beneficial to agriculture, as they are skilled hunters of the small quick-breeding mammals—such as mice, rats and gophers—as well as insects and reptiles.

No other birds look quite like owls, with their huge heads, large forward-looking eyes and chunky bodies. During the day, their eyes are half-hooded by heavy eyelids and the pupils are mere slits. They have a sensitivity to dim light that is fifty to one hundred times greater than that of human beings and, this, coupled with their extremely good hearing, enables them to hunt with comparative ease swiftly and silently at night.

Owls do not turn their eyes as do mammals. Instead they rotate their entire heads, sometimes at an angle. This gives them an air of concentrated attention, part of which is justified and explained by the fact that they have acute and accurate directional hearing and are listening as intently as they are seeing. They have a wide range of sounds—hoots, shrieks and wails that carry wide distances to announce ownership of their territories.

Although owls have learned to coexist with man, they, like all birds of prey, are in a precarious position. They need and deserve our protection and care instead of the mistrust, suspicion and persecution that have been and continue to be the lot of all predators.

Two Owls on Two Branches

This design has 220 stitches by 222 stitches. The original was stitched on 14-gauge mono canvas. The finished pillow measures 15¾ inches by 16 inches.

Cut a piece of canvas 19¾ inches by 20 inches. Bind the edges. Mark the center stitch. Draw the heavy graph lines lightly on your canvas and outline the square. Mark the canvas top.

The twelve suggested colors as they appear in the original are:

001   white (eyes, body)

R10   red (eyes)

Y52   yellow (eyes)

050   black (eyes)

112   black-brown (darkest feathers, tree shading)

410   rust brown (feathers)

140   medium brown (feathers)

492   beige (feathers)

427   yellow gold (feathers)

447   pale yellow gold (feathers)

560   olive green (branch)

350   blue (background)

Eva's painting of an eagle is not merely a representation of this majestic and fierce predatory bird. The original was executed from a photograph of Lady, a golden eagle that lived with Kent Durden and his family in southern California. After sixteen years, Lady left the Durdens to begin a life of freedom with a wild mate and raise young eaglets as nature meant her to do. The photograph from which the painting was made is on the cover of Mr. Durden's loving and humorous book about her, *Gifts of an Eagle*.

Like many birds, especially raptors, eagles mate for life and return to the same nest at the same time each year. Only natural or accidental death or the deliberate killing by man separates them. Eagles are among the largest of the predatory birds; golden eagles have wingspreads of from six to eight feet and stand over three feet high. All predators play a vital part in the balance of nature. An occasional very small farm animal may be taken by one of these birds, but the beneficial function they perform—preying on snakes, rodents and other quick-breeding animals that pose problems to man—makes their survival essential.

Large birds are generally longer lived than mammals; an eagle's life-span is twenty to thirty-five years. Unfortunately the chief causes of death among large birds and all raptors are not natural or accidental. Rather, certain persistent pesticides, deliberate poisonings, illegal shooting and habitat destruction have taken and, sadly, are still taking a heavy toll of these beautiful and efficient flying hunters.

The eagle first appeared on a United States coin in 1776, and it has been present ever since. The bald eagle became our national symbol in 1782. It is a bitter commentary on America's life-style that this very symbol of our country's independence and pride has suffered persecution throughout most of its range and is today numerous only in Alaska and Florida; but even there, though, like all eagles, it is federally protected, its numbers are dropping. Protective laws are only good as crime deterrents. If the future of these great birds is to be assured, much more understanding of their role in our ecology is needed.

Eagle on a Crag

The graph for this design has 166 stitches by 220 stitches. Worked on 14-gauge mono canvas, the finished piece would measure 11¾ inches by 15¾ inches. However, the original piece as shown in the color plate was stitched on 10-gauge mono canvas. The finished piece measures 16½ inches by 22 inches.

You can add the extra background or even more if you choose, but remember to add the two inches all around whatever piece of canvas you cut. Bind the edges. Mark the center stitch. Copy the heavy graph lines lightly on your canvas and outline the rectangle. Mark the canvas top.

The eight suggested colors as they appear in the original are:

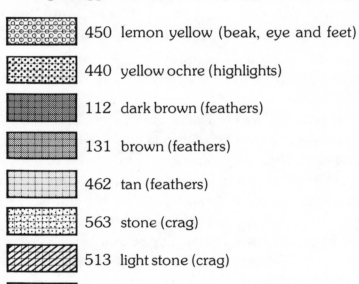

450 lemon yellow (beak, eye and feet)

440 yellow ochre (highlights)

112 dark brown (feathers)

131 brown (feathers)

462 tan (feathers)

563 stone (crag)

513 light stone (crag)

396 sky blue (background)

Once in North America, there were literally millions of migrating passenger pigeons. It often took an entire day for a single flock to pass a given point, and their numbers darkened the sky. Their wings made a sound like the distant rumbling of thunder. The last living passenger pigeon died in the Cincinnati Zoo in 1914.

It was not easy to cause the extinction of such a large number of birds. They were hunted and persecuted mercilessly for sport and for food. There were other birds, as well, that no longer exist and never will again, for once a species has been wiped out, no power known to man can ever bring it back. Twelve valuable and interesting species of birds have disappeared from America in the less than two hundred years of the existence of the United States. Others are endangered and may vanish within a few years. Some have been saved from extinction even at a cost of human life.

During the nineteenth century, market hunters, killing thousands of birds for feathers and meat, destroyed or nearly destroyed some species before the American people realized what was happening. The tragedy was underscored by the killing of a brave warden on July 8, 1905. While trying to prevent the poaching of protected egrets in Florida, he was shot to death.

In 1908, the Audubon Society's Warden McLeod was brutally murdered by bird plume hunters in South Carolina. These two lives sacrificed to the greed of man and the vanity of women struck at the very heart of the traffic in bird plumage. In 1910, a bill was signed into law in New York State forbidding the commercial use of wild bird feathers.

It is in memory of lost birds that Eva has painted the fanciful and exotic canvases of "Birds with Red Border," "Birds with Orange Border" and "Ducks at Stream's Edge." Unlike the rest of the animals pictured in this book, they exist only in her imagination. You can use the colors we have suggested or change them in any way you choose.

Birds with Red Border

This design has 220 stitches by 235 stitches. The original was stitched on 14-gauge mono canvas. The finished pillow measures 15¾ inches by 16¾ inches.

Cut a piece of canvas 19¾ inches by 20¾ inches. Bind the edges. Mark the center stitch. Draw the heavy graph lines lightly on your canvas and outline the square. Mark the canvas top.

The thirteen suggested colors as they appear in the original are:

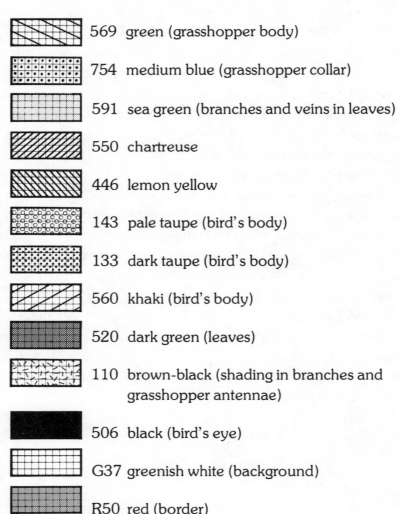

569 green (grasshopper body)

754 medium blue (grasshopper collar)

591 sea green (branches and veins in leaves)

550 chartreuse

446 lemon yellow

143 pale taupe (bird's body)

133 dark taupe (bird's body)

560 khaki (bird's body)

520 dark green (leaves)

110 brown-black (shading in branches and grasshopper antennae)

506 black (bird's eye)

G37 greenish white (background)

R50 red (border)

Birds with Orange Border

This design has 228 stitches by 214 stitches. The original was stitched on 14-gauge mono canvas. The finished pillow measures 16¾ inches by 15¾ inches.

Cut a piece of canvas 20¾ inches by 19¾ inches. Bind the edges. Mark the center stitch. Draw the heavy graph lines on your canvas and outline the square. Mark the canvas top.

The twelve suggested colors as they appear in the original are:

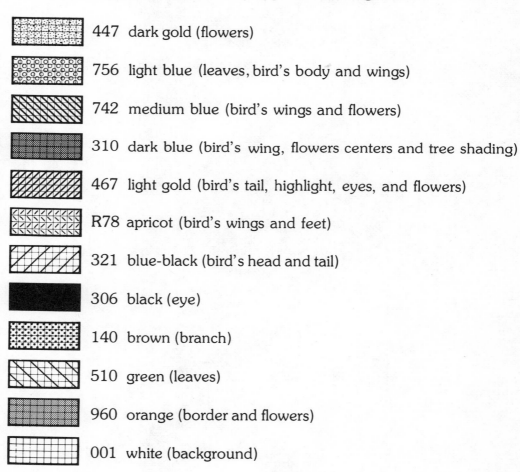

447 dark gold (flowers)

756 light blue (leaves, bird's body and wings)

742 medium blue (bird's wings and flowers)

310 dark blue (bird's wing, flowers centers and tree shading)

467 light gold (bird's tail, highlight, eyes, and flowers)

R78 apricot (bird's wings and feet)

321 blue-black (bird's head and tail)

306 black (eye)

140 brown (branch)

510 green (leaves)

960 orange (border and flowers)

001 white (background)

The photographed pillow shows how texture stitches can be used in borders.

100

Twenty
Designs
with Graph
Patterns

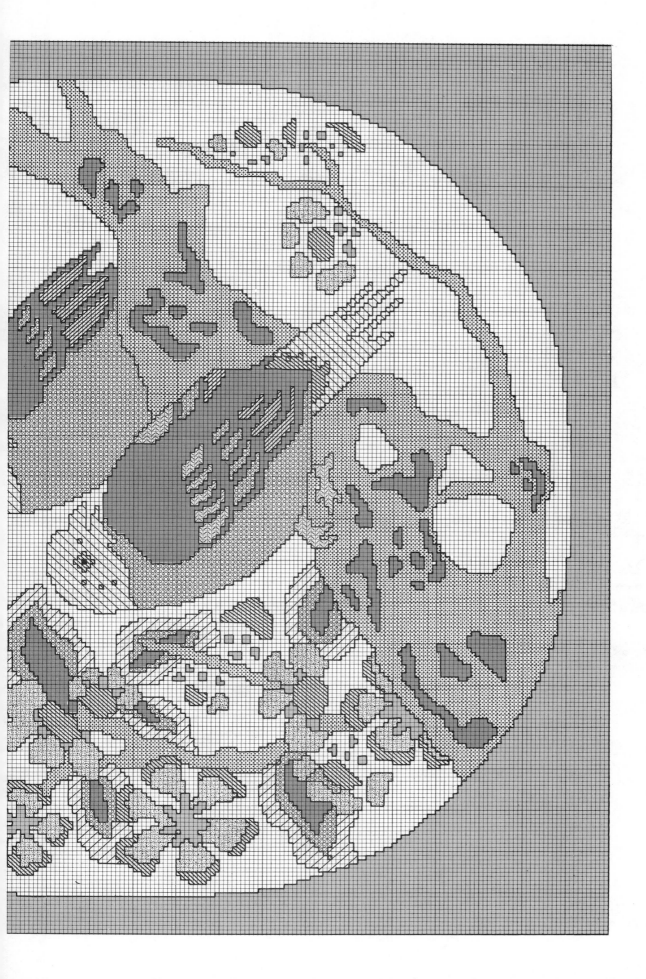

Four Ducks with Flowers at Stream's Edge

This design has 222 stitches by 222 stitches. The original was stitched on 14-gauge mono canvas. The finished canvas measures 16 inches square. Although we show it framed, it could as easily be a pillow.

Cut a piece of canvas 20 inches square. Bind the edges. Mark the center stitch. Draw the heavy graph lines on your canvas and outline the square. Mark the canvas top.

The seventeen suggested colors as they appear in the original are:

505 darker green (leaves)

510 green (leaves)

G64 light green (in duck's body)

G54 dark green (in duck's body)

143 light taupe (in duck's body)

123 medium taupe (in duck's body)

115 dark taupe (in duck's body and eyes)

446 gold (in duck's body)

492 beige (in duck's body)

260 apricot (duck's feet and bills)

450 yellow (eyes and flower centers)

618 violet (flowers)

860 pink (flowers)

318 dark blue (water spots)

570 green (grass)

322 pastel blue (water)

Y58 lemon yellow (background)

Twenty
Designs
with Graph
Patterns

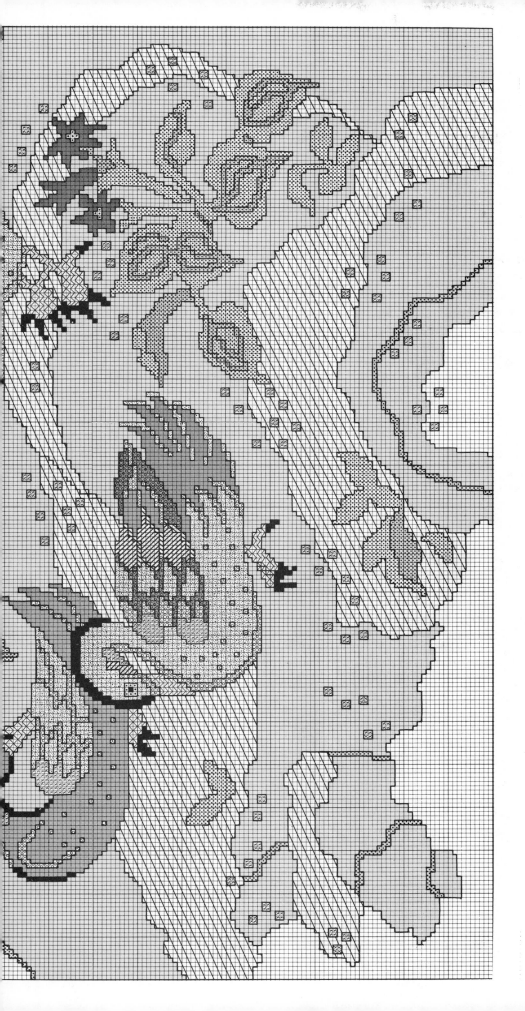

SWANS

Swans are the largest of waterfowl; in fact, the handsome trumpeter swan, so named for its low, sonorous cry, has a wingspread of from eight to ten feet. All have long, flexible necks and are able to swim gracefully. They are strong fliers but are unable to dive and are awkward on land. All but two species have pure white plumage. These are the famous black swan of Australia, which is all black except for the white outer wing feathers and scarlet bill, and the beautiful black-necked swan of Argentina and Patagonia, which is all white except for a deep, velvety black on the upper part of the neck.

Swans are strictly monogamous. If one of a pair dies or is accidentally killed, the mate will mourn for a long, long time. Both birds collaborate in nest building, with the males supplying most of the material and the females doing most of the decorating. During incubation, the male protects his mate and feeds her, and when the cygnets, as the young swans are called, are hatched, he helps feed and protect them. He will become quite fierce, even dangerous, if he thinks they are threatened. The family remains united until the following year, when the cygnets separate from their parents. If alarmed while swimming, young swans take refuge between the uplifted wings on the back of the father or mother, and it is not an uncommon sight to see adult swans swimming with infant heads poking from the feathers above their backs.

During the winter, they live in flocks; but, with the approach of mating time, the pairs separate and establish breeding territories, which they guard jealously.

Swans were partly domesticated by the ancient Romans, who used them in ornamental ponds and ate their flesh. During the Middle Ages, swans became a part of the regalia of European courts, and only kings were permitted to keep them. At present, they are reared as ornamental birds throughout the world. In the United States, they are strictly protected by federal laws and permits are needed even to keep swans on private property.

Swans

This design has 200 stitches by 224 stitches. The original was stitched on 14-gauge mono canvas. The finished canvas, although photographed as a cover for a footstool, could as easily be made into a pillow or wall hanging. It measures 14½ inches by 16 inches.

Cut a piece of canvas 18½ inches by 20 inches. Bind the edges. Mark the center stitch. Draw the heavy graph lines lightly on your canvas and outline the rectangle. Mark the canvas top.

The eleven suggested colors as they appear in the original are:

641 light blue (water)

621 medium blue (stripe)

758 light blue (shadow under swans)

001 white (swans)

229 pink-violet (flowers)

618 light violet (flowers)

615 dark violet (flowers)

R10 red (beaks)

555 green (light leaves)

542 green (medium leaves)

579 green (dark leaves)

Broadly speaking, frogs are terrestrial animals that enter water mostly for breeding purposes, although they need to live in moist areas. Their webbed hind feet make them able to navigate swiftly in water, and their powerful hind legs enable them to leap considerable distances on land. Their skin is soft, smooth and often brightly colored.

Frogs lay their eggs in water, sometimes in only the smallest container, such as the water-filled, cupped leaf of a bromeliad plant. The young, when hatched, are called tadpoles or polliwogs and can hardly do much more than just wiggle. They spend most of their time clinging to plant life or the side of their watery home. Eventually, little legs begin to appear, first the back legs and then the front. The tail is resorbed, and soon a perfect little air-breathing frog, quick of sight and hearing, emerges. Frogs feed chiefly on immense numbers of injurious insects and other invertebrates and are a most welcome addition to any garden. In cold regions, they hibernate in mud or damp places during the winter.

There is an old wives' tale that handling frogs and toads will cause warts. This is not true, although they will often secrete a milky fluid when handled, which, in some species, is highly poisonous. This fluid is the only means of defense possessed by frogs.

Frog with Lily Pads

This design has 244 stitches by 210 stitches at the two widest points. The original was stitched on 14-gauge mono canvas. The finished pillow measures 17½ inches by 15 inches. Cut a piece of canvas 21½ inches by 19 inches. Bind the edges. Mark the center stitch. Draw the heavy graph lines lightly on your canvas. Do not try to draw the slanting lines of the octagon. Follow the graph for those lines. Mark the canvas top.

The eight suggested colors as they appear in the original are:

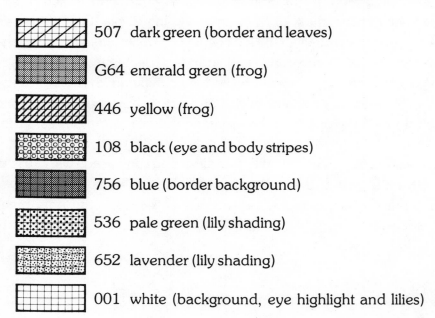

507   dark green (border and leaves)

G64   emerald green (frog)

446   yellow (frog)

108   black (eye and body stripes)

756   blue (border background)

536   pale green (lily shading)

652   lavender (lily shading)

001   white (background, eye highlight and lilies)

115

GRASSHOPPER

Grasshopper is the popular name for several kinds of leaping insects that produce a high-pitched, singing sound by rubbing their hind legs against their wings or, in some kinds, rubbing their wings together. Usually, only males produce this sound. There are more than ten thousand species of grasshoppers, and each produces a song as different and distinctive as are the calls of birds.

Perhaps the best known of these insects is the one in Aesop's fable, which extolled the virtues of the industrious ant as opposed to the happy-go-lucky life of the grasshopper of summer. In fact, grasshoppers do seem to lead a carefree existence, singing, leaping and enjoying the sun during the warm summer days, but they are as necessary to the ecology as any other form of life, since they provide food for many birds and some mammals.

They do not spit tobacco juice but do secrete a brown liquid when disturbed, which is purely a defense mechanism. Grasshoppers are usually thought of as green, but there are also brown, black and yellow ones.

Grasshoppers on Flowering Branches

This design has 224 stitches by 224 stitches. The original was stitched on 14-gauge mono canvas. The finished pillow measures 16 inches square.

Cut a piece of canvas 20 inches square. Bind the edges. Mark the center stitch. Draw the heavy graph lines on your canvas lightly and outline the square. Mark the canvas top.

The fourteen suggested colors as they appear in the original are:

419 dark gold (grasshopper body)

425 pale apricot (grasshopper body)

754 blue (grasshopper body)

574 green (grasshopper legs)

958 orange (border and flower centers)

758 blue (border and flowers)

504 dark green (leaves and border)

566 green (leaf veins)

510 medium green (leaves)

133 brown (tree branch)

438 light yellow (flower)

040 white (background)

050 black (grasshopper antennae)

450 yellow (border and flower)

UNLESS YOU HAVE HAD some experience with drawing or painting, do not make your first original needlepoint design too complicated. It can be adapted or copied line for line from a favorite piece of fabric, wallpaper, a greeting card or even a photograph. If the design needs to be enlarged or reduced, have it photostated to the exact size you require. If the original is already the proper size, you are that much ahead. Transfer the design to a piece of tracing paper or transparent acetate. Both are found in art supply stores, as is graph paper. The value of acetate is that the tracing, provided the color used is not indelible, can be easily wiped off with a damp cloth if you want to make a change. Also it is less likely to tear or crease than tracing paper.

If the design is simple with bright colors and well-defined lines, you can make your tracing by laying the design on a table with the tracing paper taped over it. More subtle designs may need more light. In this event, tape your design to a window and tape the tracing over that. Copy the design with bold and simple lines (*see illustration*).

When you have done this, take both down. Put the traced copy over a sheet of white paper so the design shows more clearly. Looking at your original and your copy, make any changes or additions to the design before you begin to trace it on canvas. When you are satisfied the drawing is the way you want it to look when stitched, draw a square around the design and retape it to the window. Tape the canvas over it. Be sure the vertical and horizontal threads of your canvas are even with the square, or your design will be crooked as you stitch it (*see illustration*).

One of the most important rules to observe

Chapter Five

How to Make Your Own Designs for Needlepoint

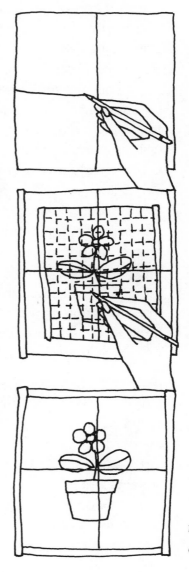

transferring designs onto canvas

when transferring designs onto canvas is that the colors must be absolutely indelible. Do not take the word of any manufacturer or sales person that a paint or marking pen is waterproof. Always test it by using it on a scrap of canvas. Let it dry and then wet it thoroughly. If it bleeds even the smallest bit, do not use it. I know a woman who had half-finished a magnificent piece of petit point and got caught in the rain with her work in an open bag. When she reached home, she found the ink used to put the design on her canvas had bled, and the delicate, pale colors she had so painstakingly stitched were a nasty gray. There was nothing to do but cry a lot and start over.

If you will be working with very dark colors, you can outline with black, and for this Eva thinks an ordinary laundry marker is perfect. If you will be using light colors, outline in gray, as black will show through the wool. The outline under areas of very pale colors should be lightly drawn.

It is not necessary to color in the areas. In addition to the outline traced on your canvas, you will have the original drawing to follow. However, I have found the extra effort in painting the canvas to be well worth while. The wool will cover more completely if it is stitched over a matching or similar color. This is particularly true of the darker shades. If you want very subtle shading, it is almost imperative that you paint the design on canvas.

There are a number of painting mediums you can use. Oil paints well thinned with turpentine work well, provided you make sure the paint is thick enough to color the canvas but thin enough not to clog the meshes. It has a nasty smell, but that goes away when it dries. Most India ink is indelible, and this can be used full strength or diluted with water for a paler color. There are many marking pens that are indelible, and they come with convenient points in three sizes—fine, medium and thick—and in many colors. But again, be sure to test them for color fastness. Never believe the words printed on the label.

Waterproof may or may not mean indelible. There is a pen called "Studio Magic Marker," and it is indelible. You can also use acrylic paints, which are found in art supply stores, hobby shops and some department stores. These are used with water, which is a great convenience, but they are indelible when dry. In any case, whatever medium you use to paint on canvas, always be certain to let the color dry completely before beginning to stitch.

Geometric designs can be blocked out on graph paper and copied directly onto your canvas with wool. These designs, however, leave no margin for error. One stitch in the wrong place will throw the entire design off. With loose, natural designs, which are open to the interpretation of the needle-worker, a stitch in the wrong place will seldom, if ever, be a major disaster.

To help transfer original designs to canvas, there is now available through department stores (or from Ellly, Box 3898, New Haven, Conn. 06525) a remarkable little kit called Ellly's Copy-Kitten. This consists of a sheet of acetate printed with graph squares, which can be placed over any original design. You can then copy, square for square, from the design to a sheet of graph paper and from that to your canvas. It comes in graph sizes 5—18.

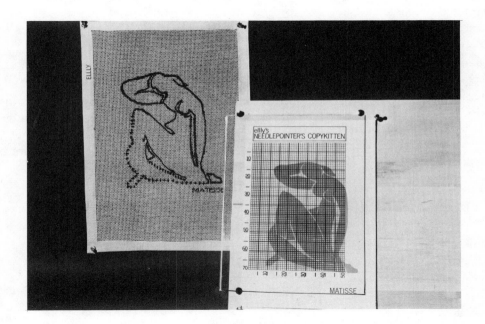

There is also another new method for transferring designs to canvas, an ingenious set of acetate screens that come in 10-, 12- and 14-inch grids called The Needlepointer Stitch Screen. It defies description. Write to the inventor, Aralee Kazdan, 200 East 71st Street, New York, New York 10021.

A new source of help that is even more revolutionary for the amateur needlepointer is available by mail. If you send a favorite color or black-and-white photograph, drawing or painting to J. C. Nellissen, Inc., 500 Fifth Avenue, New York, N.Y. 10036, they will make a matrix that you can easily iron onto canvas. The size of the design area is restricted to eight inches by ten or smaller. Directions for use are included. Write for an estimate or a source for this service in your area, and include a self-addressed, stamped envelope.

Sources for Supplies and Professional Finishing

Before sending worked canvas to any of the listed shops, write asking for an estimate. Be sure to state whether you want knife-edge or boxing shape and whether you will supply backing fabric.

Celita's
Old Canton Road Plaza
Jackson, Mississippi 39216
Retail only. Everything for needlepoint including custom painting, preworked and printed canvas, domestic and Paternayan yarn. They will finish pillows and will do business through the mail.

The Needlecraft Shop
4501 Van Nuys Boulevard
Sherman Oaks, California 91403
Retail only. Everything for needlepoint. Send for their very comprehensive list of prices and supplies. Will do finishing on pillows, bags, bellpulls, etc.

Rose Riff
242 East 71st Street
New York, New York 10028
Retail only. Finishing on everything except vests and shoes. Does beautiful pillow backing with leather and suede. Mail order. Send for estimate.

American Crewel and Canvas Studio
P.O. Box 298
Boonton, New Jersey 07005
Retail only. Everything for needlepoint including marking pens and graph paper. Send for their list of prices. No finishing.

Selma's Art Needlework
1645 Second Avenue
New York, New York 10028
Retail only. They sell canvas and yarn but do no finishing. They will send a sample of all Paternayan colors for $2.50.

Paternayan Brothers
312 East 95th Street
New York, New York 10028
Wholesale only. Canvas and yarn made by them must be ordered through a retail shop.

Schachter's
115 Allen Street
New York, New York 10002
Retail and through decorators. Will make pillow inserts in down, down-feather combination, polyester or kapok. They will also block and back pillows but must be supplied with fabric for backing. Send size for price estimate.

Tapestry
1355 Galleria Mall
P.O. Box 36161
Houston, Texas 77036
Retail or through decorators. Complete line of needlepoint accessories and materials. They will coordinate colors for decorating and will send samples free of charge. Also finishing for pillows, purses, belts, etc., as well as framing.

The Camel
205 West 57th Street
New York, New York 10019
They carry a complete line of Paternayan Persian, DMC 6 strand cotton, gold and silver metallic thread and canvases in almost all sizes of both Penelope and mono. They will do finishing by mail order, but must see piece for price estimate. They will match yarn if you send either a strand or the color code number.

Dover Publications Inc.
180 Varick Street
New York, New York 10014

They have several dozen books devoted to needlepoint, which include graph designs in geometric, Christmas, alphabets. They are paperback and inexpensive. Send for their brochure if your shop doesn't carry them.

Feiner, Wilhelmina Fox. *Adventure in Needlepoint.* New York: Doubleday and Company, 1973.

Clearly written with humor and with a wealth of instruction for the beginner, as well as many tips for the advanced needlepointer.

Hanley, Hope. *Needlepoint.* New York: Charles Scribner's Sons, 1964.

Line drawings and photographs of various stitches. It also has a chart showing appropriate uses for the different stitches.

Ireys, Katharine. *The Encyclopedia of Canvas Embroidery Stitch Patterns.* New York: Thomas Y. Crowell Company, 1972.

Devoted in its entirety to stitches and instructions for putting them on canvas. It has diagrams for 170 stitches, from the simplest to the most complex. Most diagrams are line drawings, but there are some photographs.

Lantz, Sherlee and Lane, Maggie. *A Pageant of Pattern for Needlepoint Canvas.* New York: Atheneum, 1973.

Contains 351 diagrams of stitches and photographs of the worked stitch with each diagram. It is a large, expensive book, beautifully written and designed. Even the most difficult stitch is made easy when the directions in this book are followed.

McGrath, Lee Parr and Scobey, Joan. *Do It All Yourself Needlepoint.* New York: Simon and Schuster, 1971.

Many easy-to-follow drawings of animals, plants, symbols and borders. You can use them separately or combine them to make an original group. There are some drawings of the different stitches and a chart that is very helpful in determining how much yarn you need and the proper canvas and yarn for each stitch.

Picken, Mary Brooks and White, Doris. *Needlepoint for Everyone.* New York: Harper and Row Publishers, Inc., 1970.

Many fine photographs of finished needlepoint projects. It also has detailed introductions with easy-to-follow line drawings of various stitches, a chapter for left-handed stitchers and photographs of wools and canvases.

Rome, Carol Cheney and Devlin, Georgia French. *A New Look at Needlepoint.* New York: Crown Publishers, Inc., 1972.

Shows both line drawings and photographs of the various stitches with detailed instructions for doing each. There are many helpful hints for doing original designs and excellent finishing techniques; 400 illustrations and 15 color plates.

The following list of books will provide both interesting, informative reading and a wealth of photographs for needlepointers who want to make their own original wildlife designs.

Bartlett, Jen and Des. *Nature's Paradise*. Boston: Houghton, Mifflin Co., 1967

Brower, David. *Son of the Earth Spirit*. New York: McGraw-Hill, 1973 (a Friends of the Earth book).

————*Wilderness: America's Living Heritage*. New York: Sierra Club Books, 1972.

Caras, Roger. *Last Chance on Earth*. Philadelphia: Chilton Book Company, 1966.

Crowe, Philip Kingsland. *The Empty Ark*. New York: Charles Scribner's Sons, 1967.

Denis, Armand. *Cats of the World*. New York: Houghton, Mifflin Co., 1964.

International Union for Conservation of Nature and Natural Resources. *Wildlife in Danger*. New York: The Viking Press, 1969.

Krutch, Joseph Wood. *The World of Animals*. New York: Simon and Schuster, 1971.

Larousse Encyclopedia of Animal Life. Middlesex, England: The Hamlyn Publishing Group, Limited, 1967.

Leen, Nina and Davis, Joseph. *And Then There Were None*. New York: Holt, Rinehart and Winston, Inc., 1973.

Matthiesson, Peter. *Wildlife in America*. New York: The Viking Press, 1959.

Matthiesson, Peter and Porter, Eliot. *The Tree Where Man Was Born*, New York: Dutton, 1972.

Meyers, Norman. *Long African Day*. New York: Macmillan, 1972.

Roedelberger, Franz A. and Groschoff, Vera I. *African Wildlife*. New York: The Viking Press, 1965.

Scott, Peter and Philippa. *Animals in Africa*. New York: Clarkson N. Potter, Inc., 1962.

Spinage, C. A. *Animals of East Africa*. Boston: Houghton, Mifflin Company, 1963.

Man has learned to alter nature to suit his convenience: he has become master of the earth. Fortunately, now he is also beginning to learn that everything has a price. Some of the animals and birds in this book will almost certainly become extinct, and, without great care, others not now in immediate danger could easily join them. As there is a place on earth for our great man-made works of art, so there must be room for our beautiful wildlife from the largest to the smallest. If the common sense and decency of man prevails, we will continue to hear the songs of the birds, the roar of the lions and the trumpeting of the elephants.

Following is a list of conservation organizations for those readers and stitchers who would like to take an active part in preserving our wildlife heritage.

Animal Protection Institute of America
Box 22505, 5894 South Land Park Drive
Sacramento, California 95822

Defenders of Wildlife
809 Dupont Circle Building
346 Connecticut Avenue, NW
Washington, D.C. 20036

The Fund for Animals
140 West 57th Street
New York, New York 10019

The Izaak Walton League of America
1326 Waukegan Road
Glenview, Illinois 60025

The National Audubon Society
950 Third Avenue
New York, New York 10022

The New York Zoological Society
Bronx Park
Bronx, New York 10460

Sierra Club
1050 Mills Tower
San Francisco, California 94104